"No other species of true deer, in either the Old or the New World, come up to
[the elk] in size and in the shape, length, and weight of its mighty antlers; while
the grand, proud carriage and lordly bearing of an old bull make it perhaps
the most majestic looking of all the animal creation."
— Theodore Roosevelt, Hunting Trips on the Prairie, 1885

Majestic
ELK

Todd R. Berger, Editor

Voyageur Press

Majestic
WILDLIFE
L I B R A R Y

Edited by Todd R. Berger
Designed by Andrea Rud
Printed in Hong Kong

First Hardcover Edition
98 99 00 01 02   5 4 3 2 1
First Paperback Edition
01 02 03 04 05   5 4 3 2 1

Library of Congress Cataloging-in-Publication Data
Majestic elk / Todd R. Berger, editor.
    p. cm.
    ISBN 0-89658-384-8
    ISBN 0-89658-541-7(pbk.)
    1. Elk hunting. 2. Hunting stories. I. Berger, Todd R., 1968– .

    SK303.M35 1998
    799.2'7657—dc21   98-11499
                                        CIP

Distributed in Canada by Raincoast Books
9050 Shaughnessy Street
Vancouver, B.C. V6P 6E5

Published by Voyageur Press, Inc.
123 North Second Street
P.O. Box 338, Stillwater, MN 55082 U.S.A.
651-430-2210, fax 651-430-2211
books@voyageurpress.com
www.voyageurpress.com

Educators, fundraisers, premium and gift buyers, publicists, and marketing managers: Looking for creative products and new sales ideas? Voyageur Press books are available at special discounts when purchased in quantities, and special editions can be created to your specifications. For details contact the marketing department at 800-888-9653.

Permissions

Voyageur Press has made every effort to determine original sources and locate copyright holders of the excerpts in this book. Grateful acknowledgment is made to the writers, publishers, and agencies listed below for permission to reprint material copyrighted or controlled by them. Please bring to our attention any errors of fact, omission, or copyright.

"Hurrah for the Real Elk Hunter" by Clare Conley. Copyright © 1965 by Clare Conley. Reprinted by permission of the author.

"Elk in the Welkin" by Chester Chatfield. Copyright © 1942 by Chester Chatfield. Reprinted by permission of *Field & Stream* magazine.

"Private Mountains" from *Heart of Home* by Ted Kerasote. Copyright © 1997 by Ted Kerasote. Reprinted by permission of Villard Books, a division of Random House, Inc.

"The Black Hole" by Tom Reed. Copyright © 1993 by Tom Reed. Reprinted by permission of the author.

"A Good Trade" by Maple Andrew Taylor. Copyright © 1997 by Maple Andrew Taylor. Reprinted by permission of the author.

"Elkheart" by David Petersen. Copyright © 1998 by David Petersen. Reprinted by permission of the author.

"The Code of the Hunt" by Jack Ward Thomas. Copyright © 1998 by Jack Ward Thomas. Reprinted by permission of the author.

"Hunting Honeymoon" by Patricia Simpson. Copyright © 1985 by Patricia Simpson. Reprinted by permission of the author.

"David's Mountain" by Eileen Clarke. Copyright © 1992 by Eileen Clarke. Originally appeared in *Wyoming Wildlfe*. Reprinted by permission of the author.

"The Grass Grows High" by Hal Borland. Copyright © 1937, 1938, 1964 by Hal Borland. Reprinted by permission of Frances Collin, Literary Agent.

Page 1: *A Wyoming six-by-six on a golden hillside. (Photo © Jeff Foott)*
Pages 2–3: *Icy, early morning fog crystallizes the grassland around a majestic bull. (Photo © Jeff Foott)*
Pages 3, inset: *A Colorado elk, 1889. (Photo by A. G. Wallihan. Courtesy of the Denver Public Library, Western History Department)*
Page 6: *A rutting bull glares at the camera like some sort of street tough. (Photo © Michael H. Francis)*

ACKNOWLEDGMENTS

A pair of cows in the Colorado Rockies. (Photo © Henry H. Holdsworth/Wild by Nature)

Thanks are due to several people who provided greatly appreciated assistance in the preparation of this book: Kelly Andersson, contributing editor to *Wildland Firefighter* magazine, who put me in contact with Jack Ward Thomas; Danielle Ibister, Voyageur Press's diligent editorial assistant, who helped review a mountain of submissions; and the Rocky Mountain Elk Foundation, which provided back issues of its publication *Bugle*, a source for four of the pieces in this anthology. I would also like to thank the dozens of writers and photographers who submitted material to consider. My only regret is that we could not publish a 1,000-page anthology to include all of the worthy work we had the pleasure of reviewing.

TABLE OF CONTENTS

Introduction

MAJESTIC ELK

Elk are in a class by themselves.

They are bigger than deer. They are smarter than moose. And they inhabit some of the most beautiful land on earth.

They bugle—unlike any other big game animal. They have a thick hide and a massive antler spread.

To hunt elk is to reach the pinnacle of big game hunting. To hunt elk successfully is to stand with pride—not unlike a bull elk himself—upon achieving an ultimate goal.

To hunt elk you need to climb to the top of the world. There aren't any elk in suburban backyards, Midwestern farm fields, or Southern bayous. You won't find them in the Ohio River valley or upstate New York. You've pretty much got to go West. And you've pretty much got to go up—to the mountains.

And you need to do it in really lousy weather. Elk come down to browse when the snow starts to pile up in their mountainous home. A big blizzard is often the best time to get out in the elements and get yourself an elk; they're easier to track, and they hang around more reasonable altitudes. So you'll need some Sorel boots and some wool socks and a union suit and a fur-lined hat and several cans of Sterno to pursue your quarry. You'll trudge through snow following the tracks of a bull elk to God knows where, blowing on your hands and allowing the stubble to grow into a full-fledged beard to protect your face. You'll hop over fallen lodgepoles and trip and fall flat on your face in twelve inches of powder, sending poofs of frozen moisture into the air like a smoker's cough. You'll climb down the side of a hill into a creek bottom and slosh through an icy mountain stream only to lose the elk trail in the roiling waters. And you'll drag yourself back to camp under the cover of darkness, cursing the below-zero windchill and feeling convinced that there are no elk on this mountain.

A fresh layer of snow can be an elk hunter's best friend. (Photo © Michael Mauro)

A spectacular pair of Colorado bulls. (Photo © Michael Mauro)

It's a hell of a lot of work to hunt elk. But it's worth it. To look out at the mighty peaks of the West. To pursue an animal well-schooled in staying away from human haunts. To test not only your ability to hunt, but your ability to plan (for the weather), your stamina (as you climb over yet another fallen tree or up yet another hill), and your patience (as another day goes by in the season with not so much as a far-away bugle to keep you company).

But if you find elk—whether you are successful in killing one or not—you will see one of the most awe-inspiring sights in nature. Along with the beautiful country and the Herculean effort required, this is why the mystique of elk hunting persists. Those that hunt elk walk on hallowed ground.

Occasionally, someone who shares this passion for elk also writes with passion. Tales of backcountry elk hunts stretch back hundreds of years. Later, the new art of photography developed, and talented cameramen pursued elk in much the same way as traditional hunters. Tapping into that literary history and photographic art is what this book is all about.

Collected here are the writings of the famous and not so famous, the successful and not-so-successful, the skilled and unskilled. You will read of Teddy Roosevelt's pursuit of elk before he became a household name. You will read Clare Conley's classic description of the autumn ritual of elk hunting. Chester Chatfield wraps a tale around some "sound"

advice on how to get an elk, and Hal Borland flexes his storytelling muscles in "The Grass Grows High." You will read from the journals of the former director of the U.S. Forest Service, Jack Ward Thomas, as he hunts for elk with an old friend. You will read stories from other modern-day writers from a variety of viewpoints, from the introspective narratives of Ted Kerasote and David Petersen to the matter-of-fact writing of Patricia Simpson to the wonderful tales of Eileen Clarke, Maple Andrew Taylor, and Tom Reed, who seem to be as star-struck by the majestic elk as anyone. The voices are as varied as the topography of elk country.

And then there's the photography. Images of elk have an innate advantage: Elk live in spectacular lands. Here you will find the work of several of the most talented nature photographers at work today. Sit back and behold the work of Erwin and Peggy Bauer, Daniel J. Cox, Gerry Ellis, Jeff Foott, Michael H. Francis, Jeff and Alexa Henry, John W. Herbst, Henry H. Holdsworth, Rich Kirchner, Doug Locke, Michael Mauro, Bruce Montagne, William H. Mullins, Stan Osolinski, Jeffrey Rich, Bob Sisk, Sherm Spoelstra, Barbara von Hoffmann, David Welling, and Art Wolfe.

The writer A. B. Guthrie, Jr., wrote, "Man needs space. He needs elbow room. He needs to be surrounded, when he can, by majesty." Among the elk, majesty is found

Chapter 1

TO HUNT
FOR ELK

"We agree that pulling the trigger to make a kill is the poorest part of any hunt. The saddle trip into deep wilderness, the simpleness of camp life, the association with capable, hard-working guides, scouting wilderness penetrated only by trails, the stalking of a wary animal—those are the important elements of any elk experience."
—Charles Elliott, "Saddlebag Safari," Outdoor Life, 1963

HURRAH FOR
THE REAL ELK HUNTER

By Clare Conley

Clare Conley was one of the most influential figures in the world of outdoor literature. As the former editor-in-chief of *Field & Stream* and, later, the editor-in-chief of *Outdoor Life,* he guided a generation of writers of hunting tales. He testified before the U.S. Congress several times, presenting the sportsman's point of view on issues of the day, and also made three appearances on the *Tonight Show* with Johnny Carson. Now retired, Conley continues to hunt, including trips west with his old friend, well-known outdoors writer Patrick McManus.

In this piece, originally published in *Field & Stream*, Conley vividly describes the fever of elk season.

Each fall, about the first of October, traffic on western highways builds to a peak that is neither commuters going to work, mothers taking children to school, nor families on vacation. No, sir; this is passing, shifting, turning, tear-along-the-road traffic made up mostly of men in work-type vehicles on the go-go-go.

Barreling down the open highways, trading off drivers, never stopping for sleep, these cars and trucks pour out from the farm country and big and little towns all over the U.S., heading for the remote mountains and forests of the Western States. From Phoenix they burn asphalt for the Sangre de Cristo Mountains of New Mexico; from Dallas and Ogden they leadfoot it up the pavement for the Bitterroots in Montana; from San Francisco they come hell-bent for the Selkirk Mountains in Idaho; and from as far as Trenton and Orlando they roar to the Rockies in Colorado and Wyoming.

By the time it reaches the mountains the traffic is a high-horsepower river of pickups—of every kind, make, description, and almost every year. But are they work trucks? Not at all. They're mostly play trucks, because the men in them are predominantly from urban areas where they have about as much work-use for a pickup as they do for a Caterpillar tractor. And curiously, many of these men own their pickups or Army-command-type cars or Jeeps mainly for this one trip each fall.

Pages 12–13: *A Wyoming bull blends into his rocky habitat. (Photo © Art Wolfe)*
Page 13, inset: *Oregon hunters head for home with several wapiti in a stereoview image from the late 1800s. (Photo courtesy Oregon Historical Society, Neg. Number OrHi 4371 #537)*
Opposite: *"No other big-game animal in the United States has captured the thoughts and desires and even the subconscious needs of today's hunter quite like the elk."—Clare Conley (Photo © Jeff Foott)*

As a group these cars and trucks are the best-equipped vehicles that ever ground up a hillside. There are half-tonners, three-quarter-tonners, 4-wheel-drives, positive traction, interlocking rear-ends, all with great lumpy traction tires and Warn hubs. Long ago when station wagons were still high enough off the ground to go up a Forest Service road without busting the oil pan, this group of men was one of the first to adopt them. Later they popularized pickup campers and coaches, largely before family camping. To this day the fall run of pickups is about 50 percent equipped with heavy-duty components. There are still some station wagons, too, with gear piled up past the rear windows, and since they aren't built for really rough roads any more, they often tow Jeeps of one vintage or another.

These vehicles are filled with men wearing boots smelling of Hubbards or Bone-Dri, wool shirts with great splashes of red, caps or Stetsons, and jeans—lots of jeans. Although the rest of the year these men may be farmers, doctors, cops, clerks, or anything, at this moment they are all hunters-in-a-hurry with one goal in mind, which by now you have guessed is elk . . . elk . . . elk.

As they drove, the gas-gauge needle slowly sagged toward empty, and everyone began to look for a service station. Finally, on the outskirts of a small town in the bottom of a steep valley, they found a station to their liking. The attendant and a couple of cronies were sitting on the concrete foundation studying the top of a nearby mountain intently with binoculars. They were watching deer—nice-sized muleys—that were feeding a couple of thousand feet up on the mountain. But no one would go after them, although the season was open. They weren't elk.

Small towns along the highways boom. Cafes can't serve fast enough. Cars line up at service stations, and while the men wait impatiently they stand around with hands in back pockets, a farmer match in their mouth and their eyes squinting into the sun. They kick at pebbles, look serious, and talk, and spit, and swear just as if they did it all year long rather than only this brief week or two. Once in a while someone remembers something he forgot and

An alert bull during the rut. (Photo © Michael Mauro)

rushes off to the nearest grocery or liquor store. Then they jump back in their trucks and cars, swear some more and take off down the highway like mad.

Thousands upon thousands of these men grind their way back into the mountains, and when the pavement finally ends and only a dirt forest road is left they follow that to the end with one thought in mind—to get as far away from all the others as possible. Of course, the natives of each state are out then too, doing their damnedest to stay away from the out-of-staters, but it isn't always possible. Actually the locals probably outnumber the migrants, but on the highway it doesn't seem so.

These are grizzled men. Grizzled because they like it that way. They like the feel of wool shirts, tough boots, and low-waisted pants. They like open collars and jackets in which they can fight their way through a jungle. They will be even more grizzled when they come out of the mountains. Tanned, perhaps with a bristled-face, and with dirt and ashes on their elbows, knees, and rumps, and if they're lucky a few splotches of dried blood on their pants. Elk blood. Nothing else counts.

No other big-game animal in the United States has captured the thoughts and desires and even the subconscious needs of today's hunter quite like the elk. Deer are as commonplace as cottontails to a big-game hunter. Anyone anywhere can bag a deer of one kind or another. It doesn't prove that you have any more savvy or hunting ability than the guy down the block. Moose are scarce enough to make them more or less exotic in the United States, but even a moose hunter will admit that the beasts are dumb by most standards. Same goes for antelope. Open seasons still exist on sheep and goat, but whereas the moose and deer fall short of that magical peak of perfection, the former two go beyond it, requiring more effort, time, and expense than most men want to invest.

But not the elk. The elk is the perfect combination. A bull with even a poor rack is magnificent. Roped to the top of a car or protruding gloriously from the humps of duffel on the back of a pickup, a set of elk antlers does something for the subconscious ego of a man that no deer antlers ever did. They proclaim for all the world to see that here is a hunter—a *real* hunter. That is the aura of the elk and that is why all over the West you see weathered white elk antlers nailed above doors of garages right in town, and on the sides of barns, and on gate posts—just about anywhere a passer-by is likely to see them. By their very presence they declare that inside these portals or somewhere on these premises is a *real*, honest-to-gawd hunter. A man who knows how it's done. It symbolically represents full-fledged maturity, just as among some African natives only the act of killing a lion with a spear gives one the right to be proclaimed a man.

Curiously, although a bull elk carries somewhat more status than a cow, either qualifies. One reason is simply that in either case the hunter has made the big score meatwise. He has enough meat to fill his locker, because an average elk dressed, skinned, and quartered will yield about 350 pounds of meat. Of course, there still are men who hunt elk simply because they need the meat. But nearly all elk hunters claim the meat is one of their main purposes, although, considering their investment very few could price it even as low as $1 per pound.

Size alone is not the only reason why so many men buy such expensive gear, drive so far, and hunt so hard. One of the prime reasons is there simply aren't as many of them as there are deer, for example, and except for places like Yellowstone National Park where the elk are as tame as Walt Disney, they try to stay away from humans as much as possible. Thus the better elk hunting is away from most roads by at least several miles.

But hiking or packing back from the road five miles or so is no guarantee of bagging elk. Not on your life, because they are only in favored spots. Instead of individuals being scattered widely over the whole back country, elk tend to stay in little groups around preferred areas. And this has given rise to the "secret spot complex." The secret spot to an elk hunter is the same as a pirate's map to a treasure seeker—the one he has is the only good one.

However, at times it is certain to happen that two parties know the same spot. This occurs no matter whether the hunters have packed in twenty miles or are working from the road, but it takes place

Opposite, top: *The weather is cooling around this small Rocky Mountain elk. (Photo © Stan Osolinski/The Green Agency)*
Opposite, bottom: *A cow drowning in autumn willow buds. (Photo © Rich Kirchner/The Green Agency)*

more often near a road. With two groups hunting the same area, the lines are quickly drawn. The other party is the "bad guys" who have moved in on "your" secret spot, and the reason they are the bad guys is because they are after "your" elk; they do everything wrong, and they won't leave. Although the hunters from the two camps seldom get close enough to even exchange shouts, which they wouldn't do in elk country anyway, a tremendous rivalry builds up by opening morning of the season.

Moving stiffly because of the cold the hunter poured the remaining coffee out of the pot on the fire, then slung his rifle over his shoulder and started up the trail. The others in camp were doing the same, even though the first light of day was still two hours away. Dumbly, not fully awake, he wondered why, and then remembered the other hunters camped down the valley and the need to be on top of the mountain before them to have first chance at the elk. The parts were beginning to fit together in his groggy mind now. One companion had even slept in his clothes just to be ready quicker in the morning. It had amazed the hunter.

A bush reached out of the darkness and clawed his face, snapping him back to the present. Quietly to himself he swore. Elk and deer could be anywhere—even nearby—since they move about and feed at night, and he didn't want to spook them by making a noise now when the chance to shoot was so close. The trail angled up sharply, and before long he was hot and sweating from the exertion, but there was nothing to do about it. When he sat down to wait for daylight, he knew he would grow cold quickly.

Even with a flashlight the trail was difficult to follow without stumbling, but walking alone through the woods to the sidehill pocket he would watch was worse. It seemed impossible to put a foot down without crunching a pine cone or cracking a dry stick. Making each step in slow motion he eased through the trees with reasonable quiet, pausing under a large pine to blow. Suddenly a sputtering roar erupted overhead. The surprise made his heart pound. He had flushed a roosting grouse, and the sound of beating wings was magnified by the silence. If any elk were out there in the darkness, that grouse alerted them.

A hundred yards farther on the hunter settled down beside a log to await daylight. At first he listened carefully for telltale sounds of animals out in the dark, but when that proved fruitless his thoughts wandered and he dreamed of other mornings. He remembered the guide

that he and two friends hunted with who, at dawn each day, marched them down the trail from the cabin to the edge of the horse pasture to check for elk. For a week he kept up the ritual; then one morning they did find elk, standing back in the forest where the trees came down to the far side of the meadow. The hunter chosen to shoot first rested his rifle over a fencepost, looked through the scope an exceeding long time, then missed. Jacking another shell into the .300 magnum, he shot quickly and downed a cow. By then the herd was racing through the trees and it was like trying to shoot between the slats of a picket fence at a running target—impossible. That was many years ago in remote country, and the guide and one companion were gone now in plane crashes.

Soon the sky began to lighten in the east, but the dawn came slowly. The cold seemed to be worse just before daylight. He rose stiffly onto his knees and glanced around the basin. The light was still faint and seeing was difficult. With binoculars he looked over the whole area stump by stump, and then he knew—the early hours, the climb in the dark, and the cold were for nothing. No elk were in the basin.

The relative scarcity of elk is only one of the factors that build up the glory of bagging one. Another is based on the idea that it takes a good hunter to get an elk. There is sound fact in that concept, even though it happens that elk are shot by guys using no more than dumb luck for ability. Such was the man who said he shot a bull so close to the edge of the forest road that he backed his pickup up to the cutbank and rolled the whole animal in.

Quietly approaching the meadow through the woods, the hunter was almost to the edge when he suddenly realized that he was coming up behind another hunter. Standing still just inside the cover, the other man was intently watching the 200-acre open expanse. The grass was only ankle-high, making the meadow a poor place to look for elk at midday. When he spoke the surprised hunter jumped and turned. Startling a man with a gun in his hands should be avoided, but sometimes it can't be helped. Then he saw how young the hunter was. Why was he watching the meadow? About dawn on opening day, he said, a bull elk had walked across another such meadow directly toward their open campfire and into good rifle range. The hunter left him still watching the meadow. He didn't have the heart to tell him that he was keeping a hopeless vigil.

With velvety antlers like broadcast towers, a six-by-six bull peers over a hillside. (Photo © Michael Mauro)

Aside from the rare occasions, such as early and late in the day, when feeding elk may remain in the open for a few minutes of daylight, and with the exception of that short rutting period in the fall when bulls may be called, the instincts of elk tell them to stay in heavy cover out of sight. Actually, the fact that bulls can be called with elk whistles has been greatly overplayed. For every elk that is called in and killed, a hundred are taken with the whistle playing no part. However, there seems to be an endless demand for the calls.

Of course, in the woods, until the hunters grow tired of the whistles, it sounds as if bull elk are behind every tree, and the very fact that so many elk calls are being used defeats the whole possibility of the calling of elk in popular hunting areas. Also, there is always a chance to call in another hunter rather than an elk.

Although elk are large animals, they like dense, thick brush or stands of lodgepole pine. Rules are always open to many exceptions, but elk usually stay high—near the top—on a mountain unless they are pushed into the valleys by snow or lack of food. Some of the best elk country in North America is heavily brush-covered as a result of forest fires years ago.

All day long the hunter had been tracking the herd. He had cut into the trail down on the sidehill early in the morning, and from the appearance of the torn-up dirt and bright green droppings he knew that he was probably not more than an hour behind. Following the trail was easy; it was the only one around and there were a half dozen animals in the group. The problem was to move along without being seen or heard, and still go fast enough to catch up with the elk.

The animals were moving up the mountain in single file as if they had a definite place to go. Not hurrying but steadily making their way, they had gone up the mountain, eventually breaking out on the open knob on top. Here for the first time the hunter had trouble following the trail because of the shalelike slabs of weathered granite that paved open ground. But by now he knew the direction the animals were going. Projecting the line, he circled around the open ground, staying in the trees out of sight, and found the trail again.

Elk country at sunset, Waterton Lakes National Park, Alberta. (Photo © Bruce Montagne)

By now three hours had passed, and for the first time the hunter could see what the elk were doing. They had wandered over the ridge and dropped directly down into a shaded, heavily timbered area along the edge of a small, swampy mountain meadow. Obviously this was their daily hangout.

But where were they? The hunter now found that the trail blended in with hundreds of other tracks weaving in and out of the trees and underbrush. Elk beds were everywhere. And he could smell elk, too. The pungent, musky smell was everywhere. Elk had to be close by. But where were they?

At noon, after searching the area an hour or more, the hunter gave up. The elk just weren't there, but neither had they gone out, as far as he could see. Cutting across the meadow to a spring, he leaned against a log in the sun and, watching the sidehill constantly, slowly ate a sandwich and a candy bar. It was discouraging to fail after being so close.

After a long time the hunter rose, went to the creek, and drank. The water was cold and clear. Washing the sweat from his face and hair made him feel better. Now he would search the sidehill again and then work down toward the main valley.

A half hour later he was moving slowly through the trees when he looked downhill and caught sight of the front shoulder of an elk. Not enough to shoot at. Crouching, he looked through his scope. The elk, a cow, was feeding as it walked. Quickly it moved out of sight, but another passed by the same opening, and then came a bull. The hunter had to get closer to get an open shot, although as far as range went the animals weren't even a hundred yards away.

As soon as he could move without being seen the hunter hurried ahead. He had a plan; no marvel of deception, just an idea that might work. Moving as fast as he could without making a noise, he got ahead of the animals, then cautiously moved downhill to intercept their path.

Kneeling, he waited. He hated waiting. It was much better to see the game and shoot. Waiting always tied his guts in knots, made him fumble with the rifle, and sometimes caused him to miss. And he didn't want to miss. Not an elk; it meant too much.

After a while he began to think the animals had seen him and slipped away, but just as he began to really worry, a cow came into sight, then another. Now he was waiting for the bull. Where was it? At last it stepped into sight. Moving slowly, the hunter brought his rifle up, into firing position. The crosshairs were on the bull's neck. This was the moment. The bull stopped. Don't miss, don't miss. Now, now, squeeze . . .

That the work begins when the rifle is fired has been said so many times that it is a truism with frayed edges. But the lone hunter faced with a downed elk—often on a steep mountainside or wedged in a log pile—truly has a considerable job ahead of him. It is also a job that must be done quickly and right if the meat is to be saved—particularly in warm weather. Elk are heavy-muscled animals, and it is of utmost importance to butcher them down into skinned quarters as quickly as possible or the meat will sour and become unfit to eat. So with belt knife and a folding saw or a hatchet the hunter starts his task, first removing the innards, then knuckling off the legs, cutting off the head, skinning the carcass on the ground, and finally halving and quartering. Lastly the meat goes into sacks, and then it can be carried down from the mountain.

The two pickups, not sagging with their loads but certainly with the bounce taken out of the springs by the weight, slowly backed up to the loading dock of the custom cutting and locker plant. Working in pairs, the hunters lifted out the big elk quarters one at a time, hung them up on the sliding overhead hooks, and stripped off the meat sacks. This was the final ritual, the final duty, the final task. Their elk hunting was done for the year—and done right, with the meat taken care of properly. They stood back and surveyed the magnificent line of quarters that would carry them through the winter. A bull, two cows, and a yearling. "It comes to 1,004 pounds," the attendant said. "At 7½ cents a pound that's $75 for cutting and wrapping."

Opposite, top: *A spider-web-like assortment of antlers looms in the fog. A hunter's dream, but alas, these elk are relaxing within the protected confines of the National Elk Refuge. (Photo © Henry H. Holdsworth/Wild by Nature)*
Opposite, bottom: *On a leisurely, early-morning stroll, a bull elk moves toward higher ground. (Photo © John W. Herbst)*

THE ELK IN THE WELKIN

By Chester Chatfield

Chester Chatfield was a leading outdoor writer of the twenties, thirties, and forties. His hunting tales were widely published in magazines as diverse as *Field & Stream* and the *Saturday Evening Post.* In "The Elk in the Welkin," which originally appeared in the December 1942 issue of *Field & Stream*, the beginning elk-hunter Chatfield absorbs advice from every member of his hunting party on the best way to get an elk. The methods are as varied as the terrain and as wacky as a Laurel and Hardy dialog.

W e pulled off the rutted road of gumbo mud at Pitcher Camp, in the Rattlesnake Reserve of eastern Washington, about midway up the hills. Other hunters were there before us, and white tents shone against the forest. A tall man in a flaming shirt gave us welcome.

"Pick out a level spot and drive your stakes," he invited. "I've got half a bale of straw you can have for a mattress, if you want it."

He watched sociably while we made our camp, and told us where to find spring. He had come in two days before.

"See signs of game?" asked Earl.

"More than I wanted," the tall man grinned. "I was scouting around on the edge of Timberwolf, when all of a sudden I heard this bugle. It sounded right in my face, and almost blasted me over. I looked up, and there stood the biggest elk that God ever made. He was fifteen feet tall, with a rack of horns that reached right up into the clouds."

The tall man paused deliberately to light his pipe. "'Git!' I says. That wasn't the right thing to say. I guess he was still rutting. He wasn't fifty feet from me. He throws up a cloud of dust with one front hoof, pawing just like a mean old bull. He starts down toward me, tossing those horns and asking me to climb up on 'em and take a ride. I didn't have a gun, seeing as it was before season."

He chuckled softly. "I dove into a thicket of jack-pines like a rabbit. If you want to know, I think that bull is still standing there, wondering where in the devil I disappeared so fast. I don't plan on hunting Timberwolf. What I'm looking for is a nice young spike, tender enough to eat and not so blamed anxious for a fight."

"I'll take him on, if I can find him," said Dick.

What's the best way to successfully hunt a majestic bull elk? Recommended methods are as varied as the terrain of elk country. (Photo © Michael Mauro)

"You won't mistake him," the tall man grinned. "There isn't another elk like that this side of kingdom come."

A great basin of firs and Western larch spread below our camp. On the west, the white spires of Timberwolf, Mt. Aix and a dozen lesser peaks bit into the dark evening sky.

We had felled a pine stump, with a big core of pitch, and our fire sent the shadows leaping and tumbling through the trees. The evening pot of coffee steamed fragrantly a few inches back from the flames. Our neighbors drifted in one by one, dragged up boxes to sit on, drank coffee and dipped into the box of cookies that Dick's wife had made. Pipes were lighted. The full red face of a hunter's moon came up above the ridge and smiled.

"She's a great country, boys," said the rancher from Naches, his white hair shaggy in the firelight. "I ran cattle through here for 30 years, before the state chased me out to give the elk more room. The elk eat up my haystacks in the winter, and the Game Department fellers tell me I can't even knock over one for meat." He chuckled with unrepentant glee. "Watching me sure has kept them busy!"

"You ought to know how to get one tomorrow, when the season opens," I said.

"Maybe I will," he grinned.

"I've never hunted elk before," I explained. "What's the best way to go at it?"

There was a quick silence.

"Well," the rancher said finally, "I know of one feller that plays rummy all night. Then in the morning he takes his sleeping bag and his rifle and goes to a big meadow. He crawls into the bag and goes to sleep. I hear that he knocks one over nearly every year."

That was all I could get out of him. So I asked Earl.

"I never did kill an elk," Earl said.

"But I though you'd hunted them for the last four years!"

"He has," said Dick. "It practically always takes five years before you get the first one."

"Do you mean that I will have to spend five years hunting before I get an elk?"

Dick grinned at me. "Well," he said, "you don't look any brighter than the average, if you'll excuse me for saying so. You might do it in less, but I doubt it."

That left me something to think about as I crawled into my blankets. It seemed only moments later that Dick yelled: "Roll out! There's ice in the water bucket, and she's colder than a witch's nose."

He had a fire going and was thumping lustily at hot-cake batter in a pan. Lights shone from the camps around us, and the cheerful grumbling of men roused from sleep was muted by the trees. One of the packer's horses whinnied and stamped his feet on the frozen ground. The sky was a blue depth spotted with stars.

From somewhere near a tenor voice lifted exuberantly, singing "The Old Chisholm Trail" — *"Come, all you punchers and hear my sad tale . . ."*

Boots were frozen and stiff and hard to get on. The smell of horses and leather and boiling coffee floated on the air. Dick pried slices of bacon from the frozen package and dropped them into a sizzling hot pan. Bits of ice tinkled in the basin as I poured out water to wash.

"Coma ti yi yippy, yippy yay, yippy yay, Coma ti yi yippy, yippy yay . . ."

We didn't wash the dishes. A gray light was seeping down through the dimming stars. We hurried desperately, cramming apples and chocolate and raisins into our pockets.

"Don't forget your compass," warned Dick. "A coyote would get lost in some of these thickets."

I felt an up-swing of excitement as I poked shells into my rifle and closed the bolt. Earl waved good luck and drifted off up the hill.

"Where are you heading?" I asked Dick.

"Timberwolf," he grinned.

I followed game trails up the ridge, walking slowly at the edge of each little meadow to watch for five or ten minutes before stepping out in the open. I was hunting in the same way that I would for deer. As I neared the crest of the ridge the dense growth of firs gave way to a scattered forest of big pines. The ground was covered with dry bunchgrass, white with frost. The sun came up, pouring long slanting rays through the trees.

I caught a flash of gray, and froze to immobility. A moment later a doe deer stepped into the open a hundred feet distant. She lifted each foot high and put it down as carefully as if she were walking on ice. She stopped to nibble at a tuft of grass, as if she

"... the antlers stood up higher than the shoulders of a man. The beams were massive, thick as my arm ..."—Chester Chatfield (Photo © Michael Mauro)

didn't like it much, but found it better than nothing at all.

A buck came out of a thicket not twenty feet away. He saw me at once and stopped. He sniffed audibly, trying to smell this queer animal with the bright red coat. His antlers, five points to the side, shone like gold in the morning sunlight. After a few more sniffs he trotted unconcernedly away, and the doe followed him.

I went down the other side of the ridge, finding a wide meadow that ran diagonally to the bottom of the canyon. Clumps of silver cottonwoods grew along the way, their trunks gleaming white against the dark background of pines. I saw three more deer, all does, their great ears thrust up inquiringly as they stood and stared at me.

There were tracks of elk everywhere in the soft ground. I found the round beds of deer scuffed in the pine needles beneath big trees on the spur ridges, but nowhere was there any sign of elk bedding down.

Four rapid shots burst the stillness. They came from my right, and I turned in that direction. Half an hour later I found the tall man in the flaming shirt, busily skinning out a spike elk that weighed around 300 pounds.

"Good for you!" I said. "I was beginning to think they didn't use this country, except to cross through. I couldn't find any beds."

"You never will find any beds anywhere," he grinned. "Elk sleep standing up, leaning against a tree so they can get a running start."

I helped him hang up the quarters. "Tell me," I asked, "how in the devil do you hunt these things?"

He looked embarrassed. "Well," he admitted, "I whittle. I go along until I find a place where I can see, and I whittle up a stick. Then I move along to some other place, and whittle up another stick."

Midway in the afternoon I found myself somewhere on Bethel Ridge, and thoroughly lost. The thickets of Western larch were so dense that no land-

An early fall snowstorm swirls around a bedded bull in Yellowstone National Park. (Photo © Art Wolfe)

marks were visible. I thought I must be about five miles from camp. I sat down and smoked a cigarette, looked at my map, laid a course by compass to strike the road, and headed out.

Two hours later, when I was beginning to think I was due to spend a night in the brush, I came to the road. I wasn't sure whether to go up or down, but finally decided to go down. After walking rapidly for fifteen minutes, I halted at the sound of a voice from a meadow uphill.

"Help me hang this critter up, will you?"

It was the rancher from Naches, with a fat spike elk. The old man was as excited and happy as a child at Christmas.

"Do you know," he grinned, "I've killed a lot of elk, but darned if this isn't the fattest one I ever saw?"

"How did you get him?"

"Oh, just walking up and down the road. I always hunt elk that way. No use scramblin' through the brush when you don't have to."

"Do you suppose I could get one by the same method?"

He shook his head. "Nope. Hunting elk is like nothing else on earth. You've got to experiment until you find some way that works for you. It'll take about five years."

Earl was in camp, with the heart and liver of a two-point elk.

"So you finally got one!" I exclaimed. "Good boy! How in the devil did you do it?"

"You won't believe me."

"Oh, yes I will! I'll believe you if you say you caught him in a mouse-trap baited with alfalfa."

"Well," said Earl, "I went up over the ridge and down the other side, and I didn't see a blamed thing bigger than a red squirrel. I was thinking about this elk-hunting business. It's not like hunting deer. You've got to forget all you ever learned.

"I kept walking along and thinking, and pretty soon I came to an outcropping of volcanic rock with a good fissure of quartz running along the surface. It was highly colored, and looked as if it might polish up if I could get out a piece. So I laid my rifle on the ground and picked up a boulder and began pounding away, trying to knock loose a chunk of the quartz.

"I was bending over, and all of a sudden something hit me a lick across the seat of my pants that

Above: *A cow elk pauses at a far-off sound, amidst a flowing wapiti river. (Photo © Henry H. Holdsworth/Wild by Nature)*
Opposite: *A tule elk forages in California's Point Reyes National Seashore. (Photo © Jeffrey Rich)*

made the dust fly. I let out a grunt and straightened up and the little fir tree beside me was swishing back and forth like a cattail in a hurricane. I looked down the hill, and there was this two-point, going so fast he looked like a yellow streak about as high as a horse and twenty feet long. All this, and there wasn't a sound a human being could hear. That son of a gun had run right over that little fir, not five feet from me!

"Well, I dropped the rock I was pounding with, and grabbed my rifle and shot, just as the elk went into a thicket. He went the rest of the way rolling like a cartwheel, with his backbone broken."

"Now," I said, "you know how to hunt elk."

"Yes," Earl nodded, rubbing his posterior reflectively. "But the next time I'm going to wear some heavier pants."

Dick came into camp an hour after dark, dragging his feet. We loaded him with stew and hot coffee, and he began to revive.

"That Timberwolf is a blamed big mountain," he said. "And the biggest elk that ever walked has made tracks all over it. But do you think I could find him? No!"

Dick immersed himself in the stew again, and came up blowing. "I'll get him tomorrow," he promised. "I've got a scheme."

"Are you going to whittle?" I inquired.

"Never you mind," said Dick. "I've made my plans."

We went over to the packer's fire to arrange for bringing out Earl's elk. The packer was a wiry little man from Texas, with a hat big enough for a sunshade. He had a drawling voice, and looked as if he led a hard life and enjoyed it.

"You fellers from Seattle?" he asked. "I packed for a bunch of dudes from Seattle one time. I took 'em in deer hunting. There were five of them. They hunted a week, and drank a case of whiskey and killed one little forked-horn buck that must not have had

good sense."

He threw away the brown stub of his cigarette and began rolling another. "They had everything with 'em except the kitchen stove. I was short of horses anyway, and coming out I even had to pack my saddle horse. Well, blamed if the fool mare that was carrying the forked-horn didn't go off the trail! It was steep and rocky—that was up in the Entiat country—and when she got done rolling down the hill for a couple of hundred yards, I had to shoot her.

"You oughta heard them dudes beller! They had to get out and get back to their offices. They couldn't wait for me to make another trip. They weren't going to leave that deer. It was all my fault, understand, and what was I going to do about it?

"'Now, girls,' I says, 'stop your snifflin'. I'll pack out your damned forked-horn on my back.' I done it, too. Seven miles, and I charged 'em just the same as I would for an extra horse."

The packer spat in the fire. "Them dudes!" he said.

The next morning, Dick set out with a bulging knapsack on his back.

"What's that?" I asked.

"Elk medicine," said Dick, striding off through the trees toward Timberwolf.

I experimented that day. I whittled. I pounded rocks. I walked up and down the road. I lay down in the sun in the afternoon and went to sleep. I didn't see anything—not even a deer.

There was a cluster of men standing by our tent when I came in at dusk. I could see Earl, and Dick, and then I saw the head and antlers of an incredible elk. The head lay on the ground, and the antlers stood up higher than the shoulders of a man. The beams were massive, thick as my arm, spreading to unbelievable width.

Dick's eyes were gleaming. "He'll weigh better than a thousand pounds. Bigger than a horse, not counting the horns."

"It's the same one," nodded the tall man in the flaming shirt. "There just couldn't be another elk

Tasty food can be found in a recovering burn area, as this bull discovered in an immature pine forest. (Photo © Stan Osolinski/ The Green Agency)

Bright, sunny skies shine down on a foraging elk. (Photo © Michael Mauro)

like that. You got him on Timberwolf?"

"On the east slope," said Dick. "He stepped out of a thicket into the meadow above me, and I smacked one through his ribs. He whirled around, his front feet coming off the ground, and then he saw me. He never waited around. He came down that hill after me like the end of time."

Dick reached for a dipper of water. "My mouth still gets dry when I think of it. I hit him again, and again, and he kept right on coming. I might as well been shooting into a steam-engine. I tried to hit him in the head, and missed altogether. I had two shells left in the gun.

"Right then I figured I'd better steady down. He was about fifty feet away, blowing froth and blood from his mouth, his front legs driving up and down like pistons. He was so tall that it looked like there was more of him up in the sky than down on the ground. I laid the bead where his Adam's apple would be, if he had one, and let her go. He folded up with a broken neck, and came rolling and sliding right to where I stood. I had to jump out of the way."

"You can have my share of that kind of hunting," said the tall man.

"Go on!" grinned Dick. "Do you want to live forever?"

The men drifted back to their own camps. "Grub's hot," Earl said. "Lay into it. You must be starved."

"Not me." Dick shook his head sheepishly. "I couldn't eat a bite if you paid me. You see, I had an idea..."

"Keep talking," I pleaded.

"Well, it's like this. Every elk that I ever killed, I got while I was eating my lunch. Don't ask me why. That's just the way it is. I wanted to bag this old devil; so this morning I took five lunches along with me. I ate them about two hours apart. I got him right in the middle of my fourth lunch."

Truly, the way of an elk hunter is hard. But just give me another four years.

Chapter 2

WAPITI COUNTRY

"Animals are not supposed to be lovers of nature. As regards to elk, this, I think, is an error. From long observation, I believe they have an appreciation of the picturesque and the grand."
—Arnold Hague, "The Yellowstone Park as a Game Reservation," American Big Game, 1893

PRIVATE MOUNTAINS

By Ted Kerasote

Wapiti country is spectacular, some of the most beautiful land in the world. High in the mountains of the West, the elk hunter winds through towering forests, trudges through knee-deep snowfalls, and steadily climbs steep hillsides, as the ache in his or her calves intensifies with each step.

Ted Kerasote makes his home in wapiti country, on the edge of the National Elk Refuge and Grand Teton National Park in Wyoming. He is the author of three books, including *Bloodties*, a narrative about the place of hunting in modern cultures, which won the 1994 Outdoor Writer's Association book-writing contest. His work has been published in numerous magazines, including *Backpacker, Bugle, Field & Stream, Gray's Sporting Journal, National Geographic, Outdoor Life,* and *Sports Afield.*

This piece, taken from his book *Heart of Home: People, Wildlife, Place,* evokes the scenes, sounds, and smells inherent in the hunt for elk.

Above the cabin, the three rivers head. I stood there once, at Union Pass, palms open to a thunderstorm, my fingers flicking rain to the country. Ever since then, I've thought of the Colorado, the Missouri, and the Columbia as carrying my sweat.

The pass is a day's ride from the cabin, through the mountains that the French trappers called the Gros Ventre. Even so, it seems no more than "just above where I live," and all the collective wilderness surrounding it "my backyard." Maybe that's what being home is all about.

I ate rice and beans in the yellow lamplight of the kitchen while the September evening went mauve above the still-leafed cottonwoods. Then I cleared the table and laid out the reloading tools, the bullets like lined-up ingots, the powder like grain swooshing through a funnel. When the twenty cartridges were done, I boxed them, stored the dies and hammer, and stepped into the living room with the rifle.

Pages 38–39: *A velvety bull elk pauses in the upland sunshine. (Photo © Henry H. Holdsworth/Wild by Nature)*
Page 39, inset: *Roosevelt elk in the Olympic Mountains, 1909. (Photo courtesy Washington State Historical Society, Tacoma)*
Opposite: *Wapiti country is spectacular, some of the most beautiful land in the world. (Photo © Barbara von Hoffmann)*

Above the stove is a knot, and I threw the gun and scope up to this makeshift bull's-eye and called five shots, the bolt making its slick fast slither between each tiny "click." Another, smaller knot took five more shots from the sitting position, and then the rifle went into its scabbard by the door, under the pile jacket, under the felt hat, above the waiting Sorels, covered with mud.

When I stepped outside, the crescent moon sat atop the Tetons. Faintly, a hush almost too soft to notice, the river coursed several fields away from the porch. Coyote yips jiggled along the far bank, and I looked up to Jupiter, thinking of how it is said that all our music originated as a form of deception used in hunting, that the Mbuti Pygmies and the Bushmen can, by singing, call birds and beasts within range of their arrows. Listening to the mountains, I could hear their hum, which made me feel as called, as lured within their range, as any eland or elk.

The next day, I ran up the hogbacks on the eastern side of the valley, liking the emptiness in my gut and how the parsnip and sedge brushed my legs. I imagined that this was what the elk must feel when they, too, strong and made lively by the cold, canter toward the sky.

In the afternoon, I put up targets on a hillside, shooting and tinkering with the scope until, at one hundred yards, I could cover my three bullet holes with a quarter. Back at home, I laid out the maps, five across and five deep on the living-room floor, and traced my fingers up the valleys and across the ridges, resting them at the hard-to-reach crests where remote streams headed and noting what economical routes connected these nodal points.

It grew late. I put the maps away, waterproofed my boots, installed a new pump in the stove, cleaned the binoculars, sharpened the skinning knife, packed two weeks of dry food for myself and oats for the horses, restocked their vet kit, and left a note on the kitchen table, to the friend who was to feed the cat, about where I intended to be and when I would be back. Then, with a smile, I thought that no one would ever know exactly where I'd be traveling for two weeks.

A bull and his two cows cross a steaming river in Yellowstone National Park. (Photo © Erwin and Peggy Bauer)

Two fuzzy-antlered bulls linger above a vast pine forest. (Photo © Gerry Ellis/ENP Images)

The spectacular mountains of Glacier National Park, just another slice of wapiti country. (Photo © Erwin and Peggy Bauer)

I damped down the fire and turned in, sleeping on the floor by my gear rather than in the bed upstairs. As my next-to-last thought I replayed the debate of this fall: whether I would take an animal just for the freezer or also try for what I had always considered a desire too filled with ego—a set of large and beautiful antlers. My last thought was that I also wanted the antlers—at least once and as a totem for this house, a reminder of all the elk who have built me, not only as food but as spirit, icons of home to be thanked and worshiped.

"Fishgait" was what I called his walk. Black as the four-thirty morning through which we climbed, Fish put his hooves down like a trout slipping through a flume—delicately. The frozen willows brushed his shoulders and moonlight shone on the orb of his left eye. Orion floated over the ridge above our camp. Looking at him, I wondered how, out of this improbable pattern of stars, the ancients had invented a celestial hunter. Perhaps they knew as cultures what we sense only as scattered individuals: that one always hunts beneath other eyes.

Fish and I continued up the unnamed mountain and glassed the parks where Grizzly, Bull, and Split Rock creeks meet. Color seeped into the gray meadows, and the shadows at the edge of tree line became nothing more than stumps. At sunrise we rode to a col that overlooks the valley of the Snake River. Sitting in the saddle, I watched the clear sunlight come across the continent and hit the Tetons, which I've known for sixteen actual years but which seem to own me from another lifetime.

They rise close to seven thousand feet from the valley floor, holding snowfields between their jagged spires and, lower down, gorges where no one has settled. Maybe I love them because they make the weather, turning the sky into moving spirit, the horizon into booming song.

We weren't alone. Beneath Fish's hooves lay the hoofprints of elk. They, too, had stood here gazing, perhaps as pleased, awed, and at last more concerned about other matters as I.

I dismounted, tied Fish to a tree, and still-hunted down through the timber—which means not to be still but to move so slowly and carefully that it appears that you're not moving at all. A steep but pleasant ridge, deep in needles, led my feet through the spruce. Elk trails meandered from its summit to the valley floor and eventually took me to a knoll covered with dry elk pellets. I bugled for several minutes, and the silence that the woods returned, along with the old sign, signaled that the herds had left.

I crossed several ridges, following a compass bearing through the dark forest, and dropped into Grizzly Creek. In a patch of snow, I actually did find a bear print, its plantigrade outline, walking from heel to toe so much like my own. Ursus was out here hunting, too.

In a broad meadow below the snow, I took a mid-morning siesta, feeling the contentment that comes from being alone in the wild. With an easy mind, I lay down on the grass, cradled my head on my jacket, and went to sleep.

Twenty minutes of snoozing was enough to dispel the drowsiness left over from the 3:30 A.M. rising; then I worked up the north slopes of the creek, heading toward the ridge where I had left Fish. At one point, slipping easy-footed through the deadfall, on a slope that must have been inclined at forty degrees, I wondered if anyone else had stepped this way. After all, only another hunter would have had cause to traverse this forest, which lay on a route between nothing and nowhere. Indeed, from my vantage point, I had no vantage and hardly any footing. Perhaps, I thought, feeling a little charge of pleasure, I was the very first to walk here. Then I realized that, more important than being first, was the fact of being alone—that the world had been reduced to my solitary consciousness, and that in varying degrees, we all need this sort of space, this bubble of privacy around us. I thought of my bubble going twenty miles out to the Tetons and down into the Wind Rivers and up into the Absarokas and felt happy that I had room to roam.

Within two weeks I wasn't happy. Though I had ridden and hiked from before dawn until after dark, I hadn't seen a single elk. Nor had I seen fresh sign. In fact, I had heard only two bugles. The first was that of a young spike, who whistled sharply at dusk but refused to answer my call. The second came as I returned to camp on another evening. My bugle was answered immediately and so loudly that I ran in a wide circle around my horse pasture, crawled to the blowdown behind my tent, raised my rifle, and peered over the top. Three men in orange—clutching rifles and grunt tubes—stared down the valley, toward where I had bugled. I was too embarrassed to do anything but slink away.

Then it snowed as if the country had decided to skip the foreplay of autumn and get down to the business of winter immediately. I moved camp close to the Continental Divide and tracked a bull through knee-deep snow for an entire morning before he walked across the north fork of Fish Creek and into an area whose season didn't open until October 1.

In the evenings, after feeding the horses and myself, and while lying in the stove-warmed tent, I would read *Bugle,* the quarterly journal of the Rocky Mountain Elk Foundation. One article told me that in 1985 only 16.88 percent of the elk hunters in North America took home meat. Feeling as if I were being told to go home and take up bowling, I blew out the candle and slipped deeper into my sleeping bag. Then, as the wind blew snow against the door, my bouts of second-guessing continued: Why did you come out here alone? Why are you so damned concerned with challenge and doing everything yourself?

I had recently moved back to Wyoming from Colorado, after grad school, after much mountaineering and traveling and photographing in foreign places and after not hunting for several years and feeling out of practice. It would have been easy, I thought in one of those down-in-the-dump moods, to have hired an outfitter, someone who really knew the current movement of elk and could have put me on to some animals or, failing that, whom I could have blamed for my failure.

Yes, how much easier to answer the phone a month from now, hear a friend ask, "How did you do?" and say, "Why, I went out with Hearty Jim Bucko, the renowned Wyoming outfitter, and he said it was the worst elk season he's seen in all his born days." Instead, I would have to admit, "I didn't see a thing," and know my friends would be thinking that I must be getting old.

The next morning, when the country east of the divide opened to hunting, I rode into the inroad basin of Papoose Creek and almost immediately found fresh tracks in the snow. Fish and I trailed them at a trot across several parks, and as they climbed toward Lava Mountain I spurred Fish on. Where the going became too steep for a horse, I left him and climbed quickly through the spruce, jump-ing over fallen logs, breathing hard at ten thousand feet, and feeling full of oxygen, coursing blood, and adrenalin. In a windblown meadow, the tracks became spare, but I found them again at the tree line. Kneeling, I touched some urine, which was still warm. I slowed to a crawl, smelling success just ahead and—suddenly—the reek of musk on a draft of air. Stealth became my name, a frame a second my pace, while my lungs ached with the effort of controlling my panting. I took a minute to step over a blowdown, hearing, as my boot came down, the compaction of the snow make the tiniest "phumpf." The forest exploded with breaking timber. Hoofbeats went down a gully, others circled me, and two cows stopped short and eyed me from thirty yards. Seeming to know they were safe—I had only a bull license—they took small steps and made a slow retreat.

Within twenty yards, I found the bull's tracks, which dove off a small, ideally situated knoll with a view in every direction. His downhill tracks never left a gallop, and though I followed him for hours, I knew I'd never catch up. Suddenly, I felt tired—too many 3 A.M. mornings. I also felt ill—perhaps it was depression. I rode Fish to camp, packed, and that afternoon left him and my packhorse, Verle, at the stable on Togwotee Pass. I slunk back home.

Hoping to find a bolstering word or maybe a check in the mail, I stopped in front of the post office and opened the door quietly. The hinge of my box made a squeak and Lee, the postman, looked up from his newspaper and peered out from the mail slot behind which he sits.

"Got a big one strapped to your car?"

"Nope."

"Too bad," he said, and added, "It's a bad season."

The wildlife officer in town agreed—"funny September"—as did the cashier in the grocery store, the teller in the bank, and a ranger in the park. I decided to take a vacation from elk. A couple friends from Lander and I drove to the eastern plains and consoled ourselves with filling our antelope tags. This put some meat in the freezer, and on my way back through Lander I also got in touch with some outfitter friends I knew, who said sure, we could go out during the last week of elk season. I told them I'd think about it. Their offer was extremely tempting, for when you come right down to it, the basic busi-

Though this bull elk appears to be bugling, he is really only having a good yawn. (Photo © Henry H. Holdsworth/Wild by Nature)

ness of an elk hunt is to get an elk, and using the services of an outfitter seemed a fine way for an out-of-practice, down-in-the-dump hunter to ensure that.

I almost plugged myself into this equation, but something stopped me, and I guess that something was my underlying sentiment that hunting is a private passion. Certainly, you can argue that even when going with a guide, it's the hunter himself who presses the trigger. Yet the events leading to that moment—the camping, the walking, the wandering, and the doubts—are, by necessity, shared to varying degrees when two or more people hunt together. Sometimes this sharing creates a powerful union,

occasionally even making strangers comrades. But at other times, the sharing of the burdens and the joys seems to detract from the private song that you're creating between yourself, the elk, and the mountains. And as for the outcome of this song—well, no one knows it until the very last day.

Having had to return the leased horses, I hunted from the cabin, driving out in the dark early mornings to hike the western slopes of the Gros Ventre and returning well after dark, usually covered to my knees in mud. By the end of October, I could no longer face the alarm. I woke when my body was ready, ate breakfast in the daylight, and wrote until afternoon. Toward three o'clock, I drove up Ditch

A light dusting of snow clings to a Rocky Mountain bull's surroundings. (Photo © Michael Mauro)

Creek, parked the car at the road closure, and set off through the forest. Within fifteen minutes, I saw an ear flick, then the head of a cow moose. Not five minutes farther along, a doe and a buck bounded away. Near the ridge crest, I passed over some bear scat. Pleased with these signs of my neighbors, not far from the computer at which I wrote, I still-hunted along the edge of a long meadow and took a stand at its final crest, which overlooked the Tetons in one direction and rolling parks and forest in the other. The sun set, and I watched it for quite a while, finally remembering what had brought me here. I glanced back down the meadow, and there, as plain as anything could be, was a forkhorn elk.

The wind blew toward me; he quartered away, almost 450 yards away. At the distant tree line, he stopped and looked back, and I had a moment to put the crosshairs in the air over his spine. I couldn't sit down because of the tall grass, but, on paper, I had occasionally made such offhand shots. Studying his forked antlers one more time, and how far away he seemed, I pushed the safety forward, and I'm not sure that in the next instant I rationally examined the many strictures I had set for this elk hunt, or how far away I would actually shoot, or the ending to the story that I wanted to write, or, in more general terms, what might be called the "life myth" each of us creates for himself. In this myth, for this particular fall, the young elk walked into the forest, and I let him go. As I went down to the car, I wasn't unhappy.

On the evening before the last day of the season, it snowed. It snowed six inches on the valley floor, and because the snow would make for good tracking and because it was the last day, I rose at three-thirty and cooked some antelope sausage.

I took the Jeep because I reckoned the car would get stuck. Instead, the Jeep lost traction on the final curves and left me with an extra mile to walk up Ditch Creek. No tracks littered the meadow in which I had seen the forkhorn and so, as the sun rose, I walked on, continuing up to where the ridge fell away into the valley of the Gros Ventre. There, I sat on a rock and looked over the hills and dense morning clouds flowing like rivers down the valleys. Beyond the Gros Ventre, range after range of conifer forest stacked into the silver-and-yellow bands of sky in the east. I knew that I had hunted well, and I sensed

that the land, in this moment of solicitude, agreed.

It's hard to disappoint that accord. Though I was tired, I continued on through the snow, traversing the headwaters of Tangled Creek. There, in a nasty, tree-choked gully, I picked up a couple of moose prints—cow and calf—and followed them only because they went in the general direction I was heading. By ten, I had crossed no other tracks. However, I had used up my morning's energy. In a park full of sunlight, I stopped for tea, nuts, and a nap.

After a half hour I woke, cleared the sleep from my eyes, and tried to decide where an elk would be on this last day of the season. Naturally, it was the question I had been asking myself for seven weeks. As ever, I answered it by surmising that an elk who didn't want to be seen was down in the timber. I dropped into the forest, going through small parks.

In the second meadow I crossed, I found five sets of tracks. They headed north, paralleling the Tetons standing sentinel to the west. I followed. Underfoot, the snow was soft; overhead, the sky was streaked with cirrus clouds, presaging more weather.

I tracked in and out of gullies for perhaps twenty minutes, then climbed a small ridge beyond which lay a steep park. The park was creased by a stream and held a copse of aspen. Some of the tracks led away from this meadow, and I turned and followed them for only fifty yards before noticing that they had reversed direction. Retracing my steps to the ridge and going one step farther over its crest than before, I spied four cow elk bedded in the aspen, about one hundred yards away.

Sinking into the snow next to the trunk of a spruce tree, I put my arm through the rifle's sling and waited. A minute went by. Then the largest cow stood and, chewing methodically, stared at the tree under which I sat. In another minute all four cows stood and, following the matriarch's lead, began to walk slowly up the opposite hillside. There were conifers below the aspen grove, and out of this dark tangle came another cow, then a sixth, a seventh, and an eighth. I couldn't believe that there was no bull among so many cows. A ninth, tenth, and eleventh cow joined the line walking through my scope.

The twelfth animal to emerge from the forest wore antlers, and the open slope must have worried him. Throwing back his head, he began to run, which set off the cows into a gallop.

I followed him through the veil of aspen, peeked over the scope and saw an opening. When he crossed it, I fired, and he lurched. He kept running, and I noticed the ejected shell fly out of the right corner of my vision, though I don't remember working the bolt. Then he was on the open hillside, and when the rifle came back hard, he went down, his legs kicking the snow.

I steadied the rifle butt on the ground, looked at the sky, and realized that it was all over. Then I noticed that my rifle barrel, gripped in my hand, was shaking. "Thank you," I said out loud, noticing that I had aimed my voice toward the horizon, where earth met sky, and in one of those sudden ahas I realized that over the years the direction of my prayers had come down a bit.

Slowly, not wanting the moment to end, I walked downhill to the beds of the elk and looked at the twelve kidney-shaped depressions in the snow, the air heavy with musk. Then I walked up the hillside, not seeing the bull for quite a while because he was just at the crest, and finally seeing his hind legs, which seemed too long to be real. I walked around him, realizing once again how large an elk is when you are next to him, and stood by his head before kneeling by his antlers, which had five points on each side. These I touched one by one, as well as his ears, and the thick hair on his forehead, and his still-wet and lovely nose.

I sat with him for a quite a while, wondering why he had chosen to follow his cows into the open rather than sneaking away through the timber, and knowing the answer. His park fell steeply into the valley, and I watched its descent—meadow and forest—until I thought I could remember it exactly, especially the Tetons, rising full of snow and silence as they have almost forever. He and I were part of that time and that song now.

I laid down his head. I took out my knife. It was long after dark before I reached the road.

Opposite: *An Idaho bull and his two-cow harem. (Photo © William H. Mullins)*
Overleaf: *A sentry bull surveys his domain in Canada's Mount Assiniboine Provincial Park. (Photo © Art Wolfe)*

THE
BLACK HOLE

By Tom Reed

Tom Reed grew up in wapiti country and has lived there all his life—Colorado, Arizona, Wyoming. "I haven't ever lived far from elk, and I don't think I ever could," he says. "There's a comfort in knowing that they are out there on some snow-packed ridge, pawing through to the sage. I don't have to see elk. I just have to know they are there, not far away, just over the next hill."

Today, Tom lives in a log cabin at the foot of Wyoming's Wind River Range, with a string of saddle horses and an English setter named Hank. When he's not chasing elk, training horses and gun dogs, or fly fishing, he's writing. His work has appeared in *Field & Stream, Outdoor Life, Wyoming Wildlife, Western Horseman*, and *High Country News*. He is currently at work on a novel about ranching in the changing West.

This piece originally appeared in *Bugle*, the journal of the Rocky Mountain Elk Foundation.

How the ridge had gotten steeper, he didn't know. But it had, or so it seemed. And it shouldn't hurt so much, the breaths tearing into his lungs, cold mountain air slamming down his windpipe. For a moment he wondered just what the hell he was doing on the mountain. Twenty years ago, he would have rested on a log and jokingly told himself that he was getting too old for this. Now he was paying city doctors good money to tell him he should be in a rocking chair somewhere, instead of perched 10,000 feet above sea level on some rugged mountain. *To hell with 'em.*

But he admitted that he had to rest. The ridge was almost a cliff—way too steep for a horse. He glanced longingly back down to where the buckskin was tied. A damn good horse, too good to be tied against the chalky bark of an aspen instead of beneath him on the way into the timber. But the trip up the mountain with a horse was long and roundabout, cutting deeply into precious daylight. He'd go the way he'd done it so many times before—straight up over the massive hunk of an ancient volcano.

"Surely, there are larger game animals in the world, but none incorporates an elk's grace and huge, symmetrical rack. Alaskan moose are impressive, but would you want your sister to marry one?"—Norman Strung (Photo © Barbara von Hoffmann)

The bite of the clean mountain air, the tinge of the changing aspens and the smell of high country spruce awoke his senses. He had been climbing this ridge every fall for better than six decades, and each time he saw something new. This time it was a small bit of quartz, a chunk of brilliant white rock as white as the purest December snow. He didn't pretend to know how the quartz got here. But there it was, pure, shining and ruggedly beautiful. He scooped the bit of history into his hand and turned it over and over again. Gently, he placed the rock back down into the shallow depression it left in the soil.

His breathing began to slow, coming more easily now, but the coppery taste in his mouth would not leave. He pushed on up the ridge, placing one leg in front of the other in an easy, rocking motion, resting for a few seconds at each stride. He called it his rest-step. Rest-step. Rest-step. It was a slow pace, but got him where he wanted to go.

He made the log by the time the first rays of the rising sun slanted onto the ridge far across the valley. The old pine had fallen long before he had been born. If fact, it had fallen before this grandfather homesteaded the ranch in the valley below. The outer edges were long gone, back into the earth to feed the sage that grew around its bulk. But the inner core was hard pitch, butter-yellow and solid enough to dull the sharpest axe after only a few swings. The pitch core was two feet in diameter and he could only wonder in awe at what manner of tree had once stood on the top of this ridge looking out over the river valley.

The log was a familiar resting spot, showing a gray skin polished somewhat by the hind ends that had sat there in the past. He had to laugh at that. Even his mother had climbed the ridge and set her wide tail upon the log to enjoy the view. It was definitely worth the climb. A fine span of valley spread out below him, cottonwoods tracing the looping river.

Looking at his ranch far below, he acknowledged that his progress up from the buckskin horse had been pretty poor. It had always been a grunt to climb

The Quinault River Region of Washington's Olympic National Forest is Roosevelt elk country. (Photo © Art Wolfe)

the ridge, but this time the pain was different, deep in his lungs. Still, if he didn't get moving soon, the sunlight would creep down into the valley before he got up off the old pine. But that pine felt good on his backside. Too good. Knowing he was racing the sun made him uneasy—so with an oath, he heaved to his feet using the .45-70 for leverage. The old rifle was a good cane, even if it did kick like a mule.

The ridge came down off the mountain like a hulking knuckle on a great hand. Fortunately the pine log sat at the very crest of the knuckle, and the ridge leveled off before climbing up the arm to the mountain's topknot. He would hunt along the base of the elbow in the dark timber. Never in 60 years on the mountain had he failed to find elk there, in the Black Hole. But his dry pessimism rose to the surface—an attitude honed by a life of trying to make a living from a fickle land. *Maybe not today. Maybe today they'll be on the other side of the mountain.*

The top of the ridge was broken first by a large stand of aspen that quickly relented to the tougher Englemann spruce at the mountain's elbow, then lodgepoles on up the mountain until they gave way to fields of granite. He winced at the dry, harsh sounds of the aspen leaves crunching beneath his feet. The crackling filled the air, seeming to echo across the ridge and up into the dark timber. *Too late for this kind of weather. Too dry.* Only in the thick spruce did the snow linger. He shuffled through the leaves as quickly and quietly as he could until he reached the edge of the Black Hole. Then, his steps were hushed by the snow.

It had fallen a week ago. The rancher had watched the heavy clouds bump against the mountain then, hoping. If the snow kept falling, elk would stream down toward the valley. But the big downy flakes had trickled away only two hours later. And he knew he would be going up the mountain.

No snow had fallen since, but the six inches of snow in the Black Hole was soft and quiet as if it had just fallen. He entered the thick timber and his pulse quickened, gnarled hands tightening on the stock

of the .45-70 as he eased among the trees. It was shooting light now, just like that. Not a gradual light, but sudden, and even here among the trees he could see tracks in the snow.

Old tracks, but there was no mistaking the cloven hooves. Elk. Here and there the snow was varnished by elk urine, peppered with their unmistakable droppings. At the very edge of the blackest timber he found the beds—the patterns of hair clearly defined in the snow, a few hairs even left behind. He counted 20 beds. Cows probably, but maybe a young bull among them. He'd be happy with a spike. Or no elk at all.

The old man stopped cold when he saw the track. The pain that been squeezing his lungs was quickly forgotten when he cut the familiar track of the old bull with the squared-off toe. Instead of coming to a point like the other hooves, the bull's left hind was blunt. That track had pocked the autumn snow on the ridge for better than a decade. And the rancher had followed it, hoping to get close enough, but always the old bull eluded him.

He first noticed the bull years ago, when heavy winter snows had pushed the herd down off the ridge and into the hay meadows. It was a hard winter with the snow piling chest-deep to a saddle horse. Nights far below zero, and days not much better—the elk and deer dying in the fields or getting hit by cars on the highway. He fed 20 tons of hay to the elk that year and most of them made it. The bull was the strongest, coming into the prime of his life. He had five points to the side that year, and they were heavy-beamed and polished ivory.

Each winter the bull had returned to the hay fields where the old rancher fed his cattle. And each year his rack grew more impressive. One year, he carried a massive 7x7 rack—antlers so spectacular that the old man could hardly believe his eyes. All through that next summer and the summers that followed, the rancher kept his eyes glued to the ground in the high country, hoping to glimpse the blocked left hind track. Sometimes, he saw the bull,

"Formerly the elk were plentiful all over the plains, coming down into them in great bands during the fall months and traversing their entire extent. But the incoming of hunters and cattlemen has driven them off the ground as completely as the buffalo; unlike the latter, however, they are still very common in the dense woods that cover the Rocky Mountains and the other great Western chains."—Theodore Roosevelt, Hunting Trips on the Prairie, 1885 *(Photo © Erwin and Peggy Bauer)*

By late afternoon, he'd failed to cut another fresh track in the Black Hole, and his chest felt leaden. The old rancher turned in the direction of the yellow horse. He still moved quietly through the soft snow, more by habit than design. If he were lucky, he might cross a blue grouse. When he broke from the timber, a dark fortress of clouds hulked on the western skyline, eclipsing the sun. It looked like a hell of a storm.

He made the buckskin just before dusk, and the horse nickered softly, glad to see him. The old rancher brushed a fond hand across the gelding's velvet nose and turned him loose, letting him catch several mouthfuls of grass before mounting. Urging the horse forward, he started down the trail to the ranch.

He could see the lights of the ranch yard beckoning from far below along the river. It would be good to get home. A drink, maybe. A warm fire. Then he remembered, the house stood silent now, the kids all gone off to bright futures in the city. Gently reining the buckskin to a stop, he turned in the saddle and gazed back up at the Black Hole, smelling the sage, feeling the cold wind off the mountain. It had been a good day.

Far back up the ridge, something moved. The old rancher stared for a long moment, and there it was again. He slid out of the saddle, letting the reins trail. While the buckskin quickly took to the bunchgrass, the old man tugged the .45-70 from the scabbard and jacked a few shells into the magazine—sliding one big blunt-nosed bullet into the chamber.

Leaving the buckskin contentedly grazing, he moved back up the trail to the aspens where the horse had spent the day. From there, he had a clear view of the ridge some 200 yards away and well above him. And there was no mistaking the silhouette. Antlers. Then he picked out the tawny bull, its hide contrasting sharply with the gray sage. The old .45-70 would do it, but it was up a steep pitch. After thinking it over, he decided to aim dead on. He eased behind an aspen, resting his weight against its white bark. He'd

Burly, angry, and sporting a towering crown, a rutting bull stands alert at the edge of a pine forest. (Photo © Daniel J. Cox/Natural Exposures, Inc.)

have to stand to get a clear shot at the quietly grazing bull. *Still not spooked.* Why not, he didn't know. A cough raged upward in his throat, but he desperately swallowed it.

The old man lifted the gun, placing the steel crescent of the butt plate snugly against his shoulder. The post notched perfectly. He aimed just behind the bull's shoulder—holding his breath, then letting it out slowly. His thumb eased back on the hammer. He barely felt the brutal kick, scarcely heard the boom which tore the silence. But he did hear the full *thwak!* of the 405-grain soft point hitting something solid.

It was over. From his position near the aspen, he could no longer see the bull. His ears rang, and now he heard the roar of the rifle as it rolled back off the ridges and the heavy clouds. He made his way to the horse and led him back to the familiar aspen, tying him there. He was going up the ridge one more time.

Working quickly, he grabbed his skinning knife from the saddle bags, plus a flashlight, dressing knife, rope and a couple of plastic bags for the heart and liver. Step by step, he climbed, finally topping the knuckle. The bull lay in the sage beyond the pitch pine, just at the cusp of the Black Hole. A few more yards and the trees would have swallowed him.

The old man's lungs felt like they were being squeezed in a giant fist. He sank onto the log. Gripping the old rifle with both hands, he hung his head between his knees until his breath and his swimming head came back.

The rancher finally got to his feet and walked the 20 paces to the bull. When he knelt beside it, the old man saw what he'd somehow expected—the blocked left hind. *It's him.* The old man sat for several minutes. He was startled by his own voice, distant and gravelly. He had never been a religious man, had only been in church twice—at his wedding and for his wife's funeral. But on this night, he said a prayer, thanking the mountain for the bull and the hunt.

The bull's antlers were thick at the base, but the last two tines were short and no thicker than a tag alder. *Five points. Just like the first time.* The bull's coat was the pale gray of a cottonwood trunk and too thin. *Not quite what you used to be, are you?*

A blast of wind ripped down the old man's neck, bringing him back to the task before him. There was snow in the wind, lots of it. Twice, he tried to roll the bull on its back, but effort was futile—probably even for a healthy man. Working mostly by feel, the old man nicked his hands several times with the sharp edge of his knife, and by the time he'd finished, they were cold, bleeding and sore. The snow was driving hard now, covering the ground and the bull. Almost three inches so far. It was going to be one hell of a storm.

The old man slipped the bull's heart and liver into plastic bags and tied a handkerchief to one of the bull's antlers to keep the critters away until he could return in the morning and pack him out. The plumes of steam curling up from the bull's chest cavity saddened the old man. *Maybe I should have let him go. Hell, I've shot enough elk in my days.* But this one was special.

The almost-full moon should have been up by now, but only the palest light illuminated the thick swirl of flakes. Then the pain hit him again. And the fear. Cold, unrelenting fear. A shadow passed through his mind which he acknowledged, then choked back down. A dozen years ago he'd vowed to die here on this mountain and not in some hospital bed. It had been a fine idea . . .

He struggled to his feet and inched down the steep slope, hanging onto sagebrush and bunchgrass as he went. His mouth tasted dry and bitter and he felt almost as if he were sleepwalking. The gelding nickered softly again, and the old man brushed away the snow and struggled into the saddle.

It was a blizzard, one of the worst the old rancher had ever been caught in. He'd be lucky to make the ranch, but he had a good horse under him. The buckskin gingerly picked his way, a hoof skidding on a root or a rock from time to time. Leaning forward in the saddle, the rancher let his hat take the snow, trusting the gelding to find his way. Once, the buckskin went down on his knees, but he lurched up and kept

With a posterior that looks like he just sat down in a bucket of paint, a four-by-four bull wades in a warm stream fed by a nearby hot spring. (Photo © Jeff and Alexa Henry)

moving. The rancher placed a thankful hand on the muscular neck as the gelding started on, moving more by memory than by sight.

Finally, far off, he saw a flicker of light through the driving snow. They were off the mountain and had only to cross the west hay meadow to get home.

Cold to the bone and heavy with snow, the old man painfully slid from the saddle and inspected the gelding. The knees were muddy, but he was OK. *Damn good horse.* He led the buckskin to the corral, stripped the saddle off and dried his sweaty back. Then he fed him a heaping measure of roll mix, and made his way across the yard.

He was so tired. Tired, cold and hungry. He thought of the elk heart and a whiskey sitting beside the crackling kitchen woodstove, and he felt a surge of triumph—not born from the hunt but from making it off the mountain. *Damn, what a day.* Tomorrow he would hire a couple of strong young men from a neighboring ranch to help him get the bull off the mountain. He was dog tired. Couldn't remember when he'd been so tired, and he slumped into the big stuffed chair next to the woodstove.

The wind blew hard during the night, driving the snow faster and faster, clattering the windows in their casings. Outside, the snow drifted deeper, and the wind bent the cottonwoods in the ranch yard along the river. Twice in the night the yellow horse whinnied loudly, calling for his companions in a distant pasture. High on the mountain, in the Black Hole, a small band of elk moved deeper into the sheltering spruce. And snow drifted over the carcass of the old square-toed bull, burying him deeply.

Right: *An Alberta bull and three cows are wide awake bright and early. (Photo © Bruce Montagne)*
Overleaf: *Like the mountains in the background, this monarch's antlers reach for the sky. (Photo © Art Wolfe)*

Chapter 3

THE BUGLE
OF THE WILD

"When I hear an elk bugle, there comes a primordial tingle along my spine and my attention is riveted to that ancient compelling call. For that instant it is very clear to me what is truly important. Somehow, there is an announcement that there is wholeness and wildness left and that—for that instant and in that place—all seems right with the world."
—Jack Ward Thomas, Speech at the First Annual Meeting
of the Rocky Mountain Elk Foundation, 1985

A GOOD TRADE

By Maple Andrew Taylor

The bugle of the bull elk is mesmerizing, one of the most emotional, seductive sounds in nature—and not just for the cow elk; any person coming in range of the haunting wail of a rutting bull will be stopped in his or her tracks. The bugle is essentially advertising for mates during the rut, with the loudest bugling bull drawing the most cows into his herd. But to the hunter and anyone else who find themselves in the western mountains listening to the otherwordly sound of a rutting bull elk, the bugle is a symbol for the reasons they are in the mountains in the first place. As David Petersen put it in his book *Among the Elk,* "For me, the call of the elk is a call to the wilds."

Maple Andrew Taylor is a former biologist who later worked as a deer and elk hunting guide. During the offseason, he wrote about his hunting adventures. His stories on elk hunting have appeared in numerous publications, including *Bugle, Field & Stream, Sporting Classics,* and many others. His stories often speak of how the heart and spirit are served by the hunt.

In this story, Taylor finds himself enjoying the company of some good friends and some absolutely fabulous bugling.

My bowhunting clients left camp yesterday morning and I worked fast and hard, really humped, and got their tents cleaned out, scattered fresh straw over the ground, aired out cot mattresses, took my inventory of supplies for the cook. But the big thing was the firewood. Worked all afternoon cutting and splitting for the woodstoves. Last camp had days and days of wet and cold and we burned wood like crazy. Having a fresh supply cut and split and stacked neatly in the tents is huge. Solid half day and only looked up a couple of times, mostly to drain a Pepsi. Tomorrow's a free day, a whole day off before my muzzleloaders come in for a week. A day prized! May even go into Telluride for a plate of enchiladas. Life is good.

Checking the answering machine down at the ranch house I get a message that a couple of friends are in the area on business and heard that the elk were bugling and want to stop by camp this evening and have a listen. I get cleaned up and take some steaks from the freezer so we'll have some supper to go with whatever drink they will most certainly bring. Which they most certainly do bring, and in no small quantity.

The bugling is in even larger quantity: I've never heard such carrying on. Right at sunset there's whistling from way up the mountain and way across the drainage at the same level, up the creek and a ways down, getting closer and more frequent as we finish our steaks and potatoes. We normally sit at the table in the big tent at supper time, but with all this bugling we sit on hay bales outside so we can enjoy the elk song.

We eat our supper while the peaks to the east reel reverently through the spectrum of warm, living hues. Full of potatoes and steak, in the cool of the new dark, sharing an after-dinner drink, me and my friends build a fire in the fire ring with a couple of armloads of my freshly cut-and-stacked aspen. We sit and listen as the bugling gets even better. The elk drop much lower on the mountain, and as much as we thought they were talking earlier, now they truly sing. Near, very near now, some of them, and a few still distant, and some very distant like only memories of elk or spirit voices of elk who have long passed: elk slain by hunters and winters and bad luck.

My friends and I, orange faces in firelight and songs of elk and a couple of trips over to the trees where the extra wood is stacked, extra aspen, fuel reserves for the next week, to replenish the piles in the tents. My friends will be on their way soon and the woodpile won't be too much depleted.

Beasts sing back and forth in distinctive, individual song: throaty finishes and squeaky sounds of new rope, screech of subway brakes or the sound the narrow gauge makes as it eases into Silverton. This sound too: sweet siren songs up the mountain out there in the dark—melodious, stair-stepped beautifully the highest finest notes of Kenny G. And how can these songs come from a beast so huge and antlered and, well, stinky?

We, now, listen and laugh incredulously, recognizing the different bulls by their voices, naming them and their laments: "Florentino," moaning tragically of all his unrequited loves. And there's "Rusty Gates," screeching old and brokenly like a rusty hinge on an iron gate. Twisting more tops and they say it's my turn to get wood and lord the main stack is completely gone. I take a full armload out of one of the tents and arrange the chunks on the fire, fine white aspen, white even in the night, satiny like wood for hobby planes and up it goes, the fresh sticks flapping so noisily that we don't hear the distant elk only the close elk who rage darkly back and forth like strange horses.

They bugle on, but we forget them for some time, except "Rusty Gates." We must laugh and acknowledge his hinged old cries. Forget them and we stare into the coals and talk about people, stare into the coals and talk about God, stare into the coals and talk of great beasts and why we must kill them. Stare into the coals and be silent.

Twist tops and hand out a brace of bottles. The fire's heat is small in the growing chill, and my turn again for wood they say and I just got some I reply and they say *ha!* that was two hours ago and I go into a tent and not a stick of wood left only two lonely stakes driven into the ground for the wood to be neatly stacked between. Over to another tent and that pile too ravaged down to a meager armload. Lord above, labored and split and split wood again for the small stoves and stacked it beautifully like a mason's wall, tiny bricks white in their sameness. I will have to cut more and it will take much time and I won't be in very good shape to do so, too much drink and no sleep. And what about my enchiladas down in Telluride?

Elk finally take to quiet, flaring up now and then like the fire at a sudden breeze. Elk sounds now only accidental scratches across the chalkboard quiet of night. My friends and I all sit on the same side of the fire, out of the smoke, closely huddled, wrapped in our own arms and these elk and this fire and September Colorado. This I'll have to write about someday, how we stayed up all night until the elk began to sing again in the morning and how we burned all this wood cut and split and split again, meant for stoves. But I won't write about it tomorrow. Tomorrow I'll cut and split and split again more wood, sweat in the hard mountain sun, hunger for the enchilada, and mourn lost sleep and the loss of a day. But I won't mourn much.

It will have been a good trade.

Above: *Something has caught the attention of this bull as two cows casually forage. Perhaps it is a bugled challenge from a trespassing bull. (Photo © Michael Mauro)*

Left: *"The bull, always in the background, imitated coyote barks, chortles, the drumming of a ruffed grouse, the braying of a donkey, the hoot of an owl, the caterwauling of a cougar. The night rang with the traditional EEEEeeee! UUUPPP of bugling elk in full rut."—Francis Caldwell, "The Elk Ballet" in* Northwest Parks and Wildlife, *1992 (Photo © Henry H. Holdsworth/Wild by Nature)*

Overleaf: *"The elk drop much lower on the mountain, and as much as we thought they were talking earlier, now they seem to truly sing. Near, very near now, some of them, a few still distant like only memories of elk or spirit voices of elk who have long passed . . ."—Maple Taylor (Photo © Doug Locke)*

ELKHEART

By David Petersen

David Petersen is the author and editor of numerous books and articles on hunting in and the natural history of the American West. He is the author of *The Nearby Faraway: A Personal Journey through the Heart of the West*, *Ghost Grizzlies: Does the Great Bear Still Haunt Colorado?*, and *Among the Elk*. He also edited the anthology *A Hunter's Heart: Honest Essays on Blood Sport*. His writing has appeared in *Backpacker*, *Bugle*, *Outdoor Life*, *Sports Afield*, *Gray's Sporting Journal*, and many other national and regional magazines.

Many elk hunters bugle for wapiti, hoping to call in a rutting elk that thinks his domain is being challenged by the bugle of a disrespectful, interloping bull. Some hunters are unconvinced that artificial bugling does any good, and Petersen himself harbors doubts. But when he finds himself in the Colorado mountains exchanging bugles with a bull "as hot as a jalapeño," eventually drawing the monster bull out of a stand of fir, he illustrates that the unique bugle of the bull elk can sometimes be a godsend for the hunter. Sometimes.

Colorado's month-long elk and deer archery seasons closed last week. Of those thirty legal hunting days I hunted twenty-seven—not all day every day, but four hours or more for twenty-seven of the thirty days. And all I killed was time. It's become my norm these past few years, hunting more and killing less, prompting my wife to tag me with the nickname "Elkheart." Even when I dramatically interrupted my strike-out streak Labor Day evening a year ago by killing a battleship of a bull, Caroline remained a skeptic, calling it "an anomaly."

"He's changed over the years," she'll tell you, only half joking. "He doesn't want to *kill* elk these days nearly so much as he wants to *be* an elk."

It's true that in the early years I was driven by hunter's insecurity and poverty-level hunger to kill the first legal animal that came along—spike, cow, whatever—and I did so with gratifying consistency. Friends thought of me as a "meat hunter," and a good one—though there was more to it than that. These days I don't know what kind of hunter I am. All I know is that my passion for the hunt burns hotter than ever.

"I am Elkheart, after all."—David Petersen (Photo © Daniel J. Cox/Natural Exposures, Inc.)

Which perhaps explains why I killed nothing this year—no elk, no deer, no wild turkey either (except the bottled kind). While I had several early opportunities for cows and does, I let them all go. And not, I hope, because of an ego too swollen to settle for such "lesser" trophies. Rather, I held off (I tell myself) because I love to hunt and killing ends the hunting.

The September bow season is the apogee and apotheosis of my year and one of the greatest pleasures I take from life. Why rush it? Why reduce a month's adventures afield to mere days in response to some senseless sense of urgency? (A young man fears that by going too slow he may miss something. An older man knows that to go too fast is to risk missing *every*thing.) By holding out for mature bulls and bucks, I generally get to hunt to the last twinkling twilight of the season, albeit most often at the cost of bloodless hands. Does this make me a "trophy hunter?"

I think not. I hope not. The "bigger is better" paradigm proffered by the professional scorekeepers, the commercial hook-and-bullet media, the equipment and outfitting industries, and far too many of our har-har hunting heroes is egregiously egocentric and a flawed management tool to boot. But, I must admit, going after the big 'uns is also a tremendously invigorating challenge when pursued with grit and honor; consequently, I've become enamored of that challenge in spite of myself.

In order to justify my "horn hunting," I try to minimize the ego aspects and promise myself that if I ever get good at it—good enough to kill a big bull or buck most every year—I'll go back to hunting for the pot.

But I'm not that good. Nowhere near it. Nor are my horizons of opportunity all that broad. Of necessity, I hunt most often close to home and on public land. And by choice I hunt most often alone and employ a bare-bow minimum of technological gadgetry. Through great sacrifice of material gain, physical comfort, and financial security, I've managed to arrange my life so that I can barter more time to hunt than most. Yet, even with this great advantage, I almost never kill "book" animals. Last year's six-by bull was my first six-by bull, and I'm yet to bag a bruiser buck. But not for lack of trying. . . . And in the trying lies the joy.

A Manitoban elk on the banks of a river in Saskatchewan. (Photo © Erwin and Peggy Bauer)

During the rut, the competition for mates can be fierce. This bull does not stray far from his mate. (Photo © Sherm Spoelstra)

So when Caroline calls me Elkheart because she thinks I love elk too much to kill them, she just doesn't know. Consider the season just ended.

Following a series of late-season blizzards that put a chill on my spring turkey hunting and predicted the failure of the year's acorn and berry crops, came a hot and buggy drought summer that devastated wildlife forage throughout the San Juans Mountains of southwest Colorado, my happy hunting grounds. An upshot was that elk who in normal years are content to roam scattered through the upper montane aspen belt where I live and hunt, all went high.

And even as the elk went up, the bears came down, starving and desperate and trained by years of spring baiting to seek out human food. Anyone who was sloppy with their garbage had a blackie on their porch, and the woods were crawling with emaciated bruins.

Through the last week of August and most of September, I doggedly hunted my favorite local elk holes and saw plenty of bears (one tiny cub would have walked between my legs had I not waved her off), but no wapiti. Nor did I enjoy any bugling, and even fresh spoor was precious rare. Meanwhile, I kept hearing reports about the unusually high number of elk ganged at timberline: "Just lazing around in big herds in the open at midday; never seen the likes!" And, of course, all of them well out of my horseless reach (packing a camp in is no problem but packing a camp and an elk *out* certainly would be).

My last-minute savior was a rancher friend who took pity and invited me to hunt his rarely hunted high-country spread during the season's final weekend. The previous fall, I'd hitched this good man to the woman of his dreams ("Preacher Dave," they call me, your friendly mail-order minister; you find 'em, I'll bind 'em), and I guess he felt he owed me. He didn't. But neither did he have to ask twice, since private land hunts are a privilege to which I'm almost never privy. I drove up Friday and slept poorly that night. Even after all these years, the anticipatory excitement has yet to wane and I pray it never does.

Saturday provided a near-continuous symphony of bugling and close calls enough to fuel a nonstop adrenaline buzz, notwithstanding I was unable to put together a single bow-range set-up. But Sunday, *that* was the day, compressing all the action I'd missed all season into one frenetic daylong blitz culminating in the most awesome and exciting elk encounter I've ever experienced.

Hunting alone and mere minutes into Sunday's frosty dawn, I found myself on my belly, sledding through frozen grass toward a six-by-six dandy holding forth from the head of a subalpine meadow. While his big beige butt stared at me (so to speak), his antlered end yelled curses at another bugler farther up the mountain. No other elk were in sight. I was taking my time and had cut the distance by more than half, when an unseen cow rose like a specter out of the knee-high grass mere feet ahead. She barked and bolted, and the bull went with her, no questions asked.

So it began.

And so it continued, more and less, with me chasing willy-nilly from one wapiti close encounter to another. At midday (for example), a careless spike came prancing in to my cow calls and stopped broadside at seventeen yards with his head behind an aspen tree—a meat hunter's dream.

And so on until late afternoon and the abrupt advent of a thunderous squall that sent me scampering from the meadow's edge into the woods in search of shelter. Straight-away I found an elk bed and there I hunkered, dry as a lizard amidst a blizzard of lightning, thunder, rain like a car wash, wind, swirling fog, hail like shrapnel, and an eerie midday darkness. I've always admired the wapiti's talent for sniffing out efficacious refuge, and this dry hidden nest with its woven umbrella of spruce boughs oversheltering a mattress of duff was a preeminent example. The rut-scented urine stains and antler-barked saplings ringing the bed, along with several deep-beaten trails passing nearby, added an invigorating hint of possibility to the scene.

To that extent at least, I was hunting even then. Yet, as the storm raged on and the afternoon blew by, I became ever more anxious to get back to work, to make full use of what little was left of time and opportunity. But even Elkheart has sense enough to stay out of a rain *that* fierce.

Finally, after two unrelenting hours, the storm dissipated as abruptly as it had appeared and the sun fought through to bless the mountains with a benediction of golden light. Before the tempest had put things on hold, the afternoon's bugling and downslope drift of wapiti from bedding to feeding areas had just begun. Now, with the belated reappearance of the low-angle sun, I figured the elk would be as anxious as I was to get out of their nests and back into the open and on with the show. And so it was with the greatest good cheer that I peeled off my rain suit (a man can't bowhunt in a prophylactic) and resumed the chase.

The rest of that day I recall with the clarity of present tense.

I've still-hunted only a quarter-mile along an old logging trail when three cow elk drift across, silent as clouds, sixty yards ahead. I freeze until they've melted into the trees, then do a fast-sneak to third the distance between us. At a good spot off the side of the trail, I back into a yearling spruce, check the wind, string an arrow, and wait. My hope is that those three were the vanguard of a proper herd replete with harem master and satellites. But no more animals show and no bugles blow, so after several minutes I quiver the cedar shaft, rise and ease ahead—and immediately bust a big covey of wapiti who'd been angling down off the mountain unseen and unheard by the great white hunter.

As the evening progresses, elk continue to slip across the narrow slash ahead and behind me, always just out of range. Hope flowers briefly when I'm pinned down by three unseen bugling bulls, all less than a hundred yards one from another and me. But in the end, not a one of the boastful bastards proves willing to step into the open and show himself. After a frustrating half-hour of cow calling, I decide to quit calling and try to sneak to a position directly across the lane from the nearest bull, then resume calling in hopes of coaxing the shy fellow the last few steps into the open. I do the sneak, but apparently not sneakily enough. The bull slips silently away.

Since attempting to close to bow range with either of the two remaining buglers would require crossing the open lane right under their eyes, then pulling off a downwind stalk (a bowhunting oxymoron), I make the rash decision to abandon them both in favor of continuing along the trail toward the distant beckoning voice of yet a fourth bull. Maybe this lone beast will be bolder than the first three, all blow and no show. Only an hour of daylight remains, and a fresh kettleful of clouds is on the boil up along the Continental Divide. Hardly encouraging.

Onward. I slink silently down the sodden trail until I'm within a hundred yards of the deep-throated singer lurking unseen back in the darkening woods. The wind is kicking up as the new squall approaches, gusting and jiving and nixing any possibility of getting steadily downwind of the bull. Making the most of what I have to work with, I weave among the trees until I find a set-up with a waist-high blow-down log in front, a screen of saplings behind and a super-highway of an elk trail passing just below and angling off toward the competition. Here I make my stand: I kneel, drop my pack, nock a shaft, adjust my camo face mask, and call.

The bull bugles immediately in reply, his husky voice reverberating through the forest like a megaphone in an empty warehouse. But he makes no move to come. Again I mew and chirp. Again he bugles excitedly but refuses to budge; he must be with cows. Time to sail a different tack.

I've grown increasingly chary of bugling over the years, having had it push away more big bulls than it's ever pulled in. But the clock is ticking and the storm is threatening a second act and I've got a bull as hot as a jalapeño and close enough to shout at but ignoring my cow calls and frankly I'm desperate. So I uncoil my grunt tube and bring it to my chapped lips and cut the old boy off midway through his next bugle with a saxophone blast of my own.

And the woods fall sickeningly silent.

But not for long. When I bugle a second time, appending some vulgar grunts to the end, all hell cuts loose, the bull screaming back his rage, hooving the ground and horning trees to create a cacophony of hollow knocks that echo eerily through the forest gloom.

He's coming.

Where before stood only trees, now towers such an elk that I nearly faint in awe. The bull I killed last year measured 300+ inches, yet those monstrous horns would nest cleanly inside these.

I bugle again and the bull stabs his heavy eye guards into the nearest tree and tries to yank up the foot-thick fir by its roots. Failing that, he rakes, bugles, grunts, slobbers, urinates, and stomps the muddy earth into a passion soup. It seems appropriate that the heavens pick this instant to go ballistic. Lightning flashes so close I can smell burnt ozone. Thunder shakes the ground and the green-black heavens rip open and pour.

And here I hunker, transfixed by this incredible creature, paralyzed by this quintessence of elkness, mesmerized by the rhythmic heave and fall of his massive chest. This is the tensest, most dramatic, and downright ethereal hunting experience I've ever known and I struggle to maintain some small semblance of self-control. Yet there's an even greater enemy than adrenaline to overcome—icy rain and wind are chilling me to the spleen. If something doesn't give soon, I'll be plumb froze out.

A minute creeps by and still my heart booms like a timpani. Two minutes. I continue trading insults with the hung-up bull, now standing broad-

"When I bugle a second time, appending some vulgar grunts to the end, all hell cuts loose, the bull screaming back his rage, hooving the ground and horning the trees to create a cacophony of hollow knocks that echo eerily through the forest gloom."—David Petersen (Photo © Daniel J. Cox/Natural Exposures, Inc.)

side at forty yards with his chest behind a bush and staring arrows my way, growing suspicious.

Meanwhile, I'm getting drenched and colder and more rigid by the moment. Time for another rash decision: I ease my bow to the ground beside me and fish in my daypack for my rain jacket. I find it and cower low as possible and attempt to worm into the damp clingy garment without the elk noticing. Fat chance under the best of circumstances. No chance in this instance, since the cheapskate manufacturer camouflaged only the outside and made the liner solid light beige.

While I'm wrestling with the jacket, all hope fades and I silently rehearse a farewell salute to the alerted fleeing bull: "To hell with you!" I'll yell after him as he goes. "I'm not dying of hypothermia for no stinkin' little Bambi bull the likes of you!"

Incredibly, the bull *doesn't* flee, but screams his harshest bugle yet and starts forward along the game trail. Holy Moses, he must have taken the beige of the jacket liner for the rump of another elk! I've accidentally *decoyed* him!

This godsend of unearned luck continues as the approaching bull hauls up behind a huge fat fir with antler tines sticking out everywhere but head and eyes and chest all hidden. I seize the moment to snatch up my bow and winch it back to full draw, somehow managing it without knocking the arrow off the shelf.

My most pressing worry now is that the bull will hold behind that tree longer than I can hold sixty pounds of zero-let-off recurve at full cock; the deep-chilled muscles of my middle-aged shoulders are already cramping, and my arms are beginning to tremble.

But my crazy luck persists as the bull steps forward, into the open, stopping broadside at eighteen yards. At the same instant, the storm hits its apogee: lightning strobing in blinding flashes, thunder booming and grumbling, wind howling and lashing the trees, icy rain hammering my skull and trickling down my aching spine.

Ignoring all of this, my red-eyed opponent bugles again and glares. The tension is palpable; the denouement approaches. . . .

Seemingly of their own will, my near-numb fingers relax their hold on the bowstring and I watch in disbelief as the yellow-fletched wood shaft sails smartly over the bull's broad back.

Like a man just told he has only days left to live, my first reaction is denial: I *can't* have missed. I've been a bowhunter most of my life and I practice long and diligently to assure accuracy in even the most stressful situations. Last year's arrow, released from a pulse-pounding thirteen yards, tipped its target's heart and vented both lungs. Yet, I've just missed a bull big as a locomotive, broadside and close.

Why?

Lurching from denial to rationalization, I consider in turn the distractions of cold and rain, lightning and thunder; the grabby wet leather of my shooting glove; the rain-wilted feathers of my arrow's fletching; the plastic bulge of rainjacket on my left arm that could have fouled the string; my hammering heart; the blustering wind; and my rigor-mortised muscles.

But even as I search for an out, I know the fault lies within. I missed because the bull was knocking on the door to my soul and I opened and let him in. Spellbound, I committed the cardinal sin of instinctive shooting, "shotgunning" the whole animal rather than concentrating on one tiny tuft of chest hair and blocking out all the rest. Call it buck fever. Call it wapiti voodoo. But never call it quits.

At the shot, the bull flinches off a ways, but a quick cow call stops him behind a twisted tangle of trees deep in the gathering gloom. Like a convict spared at the last second from the gallows, my emotions surge from despair to elation: Here's my chance to sneak another arrow onto the string and call him back for a rematch. But even as I dare think these hopeful thoughts, the bull wheels and trots away. As I watch him go, I feel like I could die.

Now, a few days down the line, I feel some better. The pain of having missed a "sure" shot is fading and I've come to see the golden lining—that a clean miss is a blessing compared to the tragedy of a poor hit, and because of that clean miss the great glaring beast is *still out there*. Even as I scribble these thoughts, even as you consider them, the magic lives on.

I'll think about all of this often through the long

A Yellowstone National Park bull. (Photo © Jeffrey Rich)

Above: *A six-by-six Rocky Mountain elk with velvety antlers up to his haunches in a river. (Photo © Bob Sisk/The Green Agency)*
Opposite: *Autumn is the time of the rut, though this bull is driven by instinct rather than the colorful change of seasons. (Photo © John W. Herbst)*

months to come, before I can hunt again, and it will help. While I sit in my wood-warmed cabin whiling the winter away—feasting on road-killed venison, sipping Tennessee straight, and growing softer by the day—he remains *out there*, hard and real and pure as new-fallen snow. Out there, him and all his clan, growing stronger by the day, awaiting my return. Awaiting yours.

For the man or woman blessed and cursed with a hunter's heart, leaving the woods at season's end is like a soldier leaving a lover he knows he won't see again for crushing long months—maybe never, as so many things can happen. For me, the pain of this annual parting is real, an ulcerous ache burning deep in my chest. No wonder the ancients viewed the heart, not the head, as the seat of love and desire.

Love and longing. Opportunities lost. The tumultuous passions of the soul. The heart-cracking irony of good times recalled is that the more precious the experience remembered, the more painful its memory—because it reminds us that those times, those relationships, those possibilities—are gone. Forever.

But how can I explain such feelings to others when I can't even sort them out for myself? How was it my old friend Ed Abbey put it? *In my imagination . . . desire and love and death lead through the wilderness of human life into the wilderness of the natural world—and continue, round and round, perhaps forever, back again to wherever it is we began.*

I hunt elk because I love both the animals and the crinkled-up landscapes they animate. And I kill them—when I'm ready and when they allow it—in order to bring a bit of their magic, wildness, and freedom into my body, my home, and my life.

I am Elkheart, after all.

Chapter 4

ELK CAMP

"Daylight came reluctantly. Numb with cold, we scanned the mountain slopes. But neither sunlight nor shadow revealed anything larger than a vagrant raven. We were discussing our next move when suddenly we heard the shrill whistle of a bull elk just below us. Then a second bull bugled, and a few minutes later a third one challenged. I wasn't cold anymore."
—*Erwin A. Bauer in "Bugle Call for a Bull Elk," Field & Stream, 1963*

Above: *An elk cow and calf gingerly stroll across Yellowstone National Park's Mammoth Hot Springs. (Photo © Henry H. Holdsworth/Wild by Nature)*

Right: *A Rocky Mountain cow peers over some foliage. (Photo © David Welling)*

the lead ropes of the pack horses, and head up the trail, time runs backward in its course. Those who do not understand that do not understand elk hunting.

This trip, Bob and Randy hiked in ahead of us to our camp in the high country; Bill and I hunted an earlier season and are serving as "outfitters" for this hunt. The horses are well-conditioned from a summer of work, and they climb steadily without needing rest. Bill whistles as he and Keno, his beautiful black thoroughbred, lead the way up the switchbacked trail. We top out at the lake at 3:00 p.m., having covered ten miles with a 2,500-foot change in elevation in three hours.

We sit silently for some time; the only sound is the breathing of the horses and the occasional creak of saddle leather.

A mile from camp we spot smoke rising from the stove pipe—a sure sign that there is hot coffee on the stove. A cup of hot coffee with perhaps a dash of good cheer will be nice after a twenty-five-mile ride. That thought fills our heads during the last mile, as our world begins to turn more and more on simple things.

27 October 1988, Morning: Bill and I arise well before dawn to feed the hunters and put them on their way. The world is awash in moonlight so bright that the stars are barely visible. The granite outcrops above gleam white as snow. Frost has come during the night, and the moonlight glistens off the ice crystals coating the elk sedge in the meadow. The soft clanging of bells draws my eyes to where the horses graze, 250 yards above camp but clearly visible in the moonlight. Their breath leaves clouds of shining fog in the moonlit air, and the big dipper has made a half turn around the north star since bedtime last night.

Evening: Bob and Randy return to camp tired and without elk, but they talk of the glorious day and what they have seen. They don't speak of what they have felt—to do so would not be within the code. But we know.

They head for their tent early, and Bill and I savor one last coffee and rum before we too seek our warm sleeping bags. As I lie there waiting for sleep, I begin to list the things I can hear: the horse bells, a saw-whet owl, the popping of the cooling sheepherder's stove, Bob's soft snoring from the other tent, and a rock rolling from the slope above, giving my imagination license to visualize a big bull elk moving across the high slope in the moonlight. They are all good sounds. They will do to sleep on.

27 October 1988, Morning: Bob and Randy set out in the darkness, intending to be halfway to the pass by daybreak. Their flashlights dance together as they work their way cross country to the trail. As we watch the swinging beams disappear from view, we pour another cup of coffee and conclude that packing and guiding enthusiastic hunters may be more fun than hunting. It is certainly more comfortable on cold mornings.

We watch as the sun gradually steals the night from the moon. By 10 a.m., the sunlight pours directly into the valley where our camp sits, and the temperature comes up 30 degrees in less than an hour. My morning is spent on camp chores, tending horses, and listening to Bill recount mountain man stories of the 1930s in southwest Oregon. I have heard the stories before, but they are good stories—a pleasure for me to hear and for him to tell.

Shortly before noon Randy ambles into camp without having seen an elk and convinced that "if there were any elk here we've moved them out." About that time, Bob can be seen walking across the flat with a big grin on his face and blood obvious on his jeans. Bill allows as how "he has either killed an elk or cut his own throat."

Bob reports that he has killed a four-point bull just below the lake and has him skinned out. Bill and I saddle horses while Bob has coffee and regales Randy with a blow-by-blow of the hunt. We are able to ride the horses right up to the elk, so we can load the quarters directly onto the pack horses. In looking at the elk we discover that another hunter had a chance at this bull and barely missed. A bullet has cut a groove on the inside of the right antler about two inches above the skull. One hunter's sad luck is another's good fortune.

The evening ritual is completed with the traditional supper of liver and heart prepared in whatever traditional manner the camp cook inherits from a mentor from the past. I am the cook in this camp and follow the methods my grandfather and my

Above: *Elk sign: an aspen scarred from repeated elk bites. (Photo © Henry H. Holdsworth/Wild by Nature)*

Right: *With ice crystals clinging to the grass around him, a bull elk has found a place to rest for awhile. (Photo © Jeff Foott)*

father evolved in preparing countless meals of the heart and liver of whitetail and mule deer bucks taken in Texas. Adequate amounts, evenly divided, of cubes of heart and liver are rolled in flour and fried—preferably in bacon grease—and then buried in onions that have been sliced and sautéed in butter, until the meat is tender, or the drinks run out, or hunger prevails—whichever comes first. If all three circumstances occur more or less simultaneously, so much the better.

It is a happy camp. The ritual is done. The never-ending circle of life and death, of reunion with the earth, is complete for this time. We are content.

30 October 1988: We are ready to move two hours after daylight; the hunt is over, and there seems little inclination to linger. The trail seems long in the diminishing glow from the hunt. We pause at the juncture of the upper trail, and without warning, Bill's horse explodes sideways away from a white rock that must have seemed to him something large and terrible. The lurch has Bill half out of the saddle and the pack horses bolt ahead on the left side, wrapping him in the lead rope. Bill hangs on too long and comes loose from the saddle after four horses are running. He lands face first in the meadow and turns two flips and lies still. It comes to me that he is dead. And, strangely enough, that if he is, it would be as he wanted it.

I ride to him, dismount, and ask if he can move his feet. He can. I tell him not to move, tie my horses, and catch and tie his. By this time, he is sitting up trying to get both eyes pointed the same way. He sorts through things, one bone and one joint at a time, and decides everything is OK. He makes the concession that I can boost him onto his horse and lead the rest of the way to the truck. By the time we reach the truck he is convinced that he can drive the three and a half hours back to town. And he does. The man is seventy-five years old! Tough. Maybe not too smart sometimes, but tough!

16 October 1991: I walk out of the office at 8:45 a.m. with six calls from the media and two calls from Congressmen all requesting return calls. There are only five days left in our cow elk season and there must be priorities.

A mile or so up the trail, with the horses lined out and the packs riding easy, the old feeling of escape from (or to—I can never tell) the "real world" comes over me.

By the time we reach the pass, the wind is blowing a gale. The trails are powder dry, and the volcanic ash stirred up by the horses's feet is whipped by the wind into a cloud of ash. Trees are crashing to the ground, and it does not set the mind at ease to look up at trees swaying in the wind with tops snapping off and being tossed by the wind. We reach the camp about thirty minutes after dark; the wind is blowing even more determinedly here near the timber line. Putting up the tent is an exercise in patience and determination, but the alternative is lying under a tarp all night and praying that the wind will not bring along rain or snow before morning. After nearly an hour, we have the tent up and tightly staked. The night is pitch black as Bill tends the horses and I scramble for enough wood to last the night and the morning. Once we are both inside the tent with everything battened down, the stove works its magic, and we feel warm and secure in spite of the wind howling outside and the periodic shuddering of the tent from blast after blast of wind.

In the morning we move off in different directions in search of a fat cow elk to be killed on level ground where it's easy to retrieve with a horse. Or at least that is our admonition to one another. The rule of the trail is a simple one—don't hunt in excessively rugged places and you won't kill an elk there.

Just after dawn I can hear two groups of coyotes singing back and forth to one another from across the river. I work along the slope toward the creek until I find a perfect spot in the edge of a spruce stand with a large opening below. The wind brought cold with it to put an end to Indian Summer, and a small warming fire feels good. The breeze is upslope and carries the smoke into the spruce stand behind me. Warm and comfortable, I begin to doze. Then I sense movement above me and hear a twig break. Whatever is there is close, and I turn slowly with rifle at the ready.

Not fifty yards away is a five-point bull elk with head up and nose into the wind. He's trailing the wood smoke. I can't see any cows with him, so I concentrate on him as he comes yet closer. If he can smell the wood smoke, why can't he smell me? Perhaps the smoke masks my odor; perhaps he has never

Above: *A beefy, majestic bull seems to lose some of his regal presence when short one antler, which was probably broken off in a duel or while rubbing against a tree. (Photo © Daniel J. Cox/Natural Exposures, Inc.)*
Overleaf: *An elk herd in a snowy Ontario woods. (Photo © Doug Locke)*

scented a man before.

He stops and looks and listens. I have the rifle aimed at him now with the crosshairs of the four-power scope centered on his nose. He is simply magnificent in his new yellow winter coat, the antlers perfectly symmetrical with the dark shafts and ivory tips. The wind has shifted now, and I can smell his musky urine smell. He is maleness and wildness all mixed into one. He is the essence of this place.

Now he sees me—but he's not sure. Through the scope I can see his pre-orbital glands open as his eyes open even wider. The wind shifts again; this time he picks out my scent and dives for cover. I do not see him again, but can hear him for more than fif-

teen minutes as he climbs out over the top to the lake. I hope he remembers that trailing wood smoke may lead to a hunter. I would like to see him above the camp on another day in another year. He, and others like him, really are the essence of this place.

Wind moves here and there in the large drainage with a sound like a train heard from afar. The sound builds and then dies with a whimper, only to rise and die over and over throughout the day. Chipmunks run here and there to the tops of granite boulders, either to take a look around or to establish their territorial prerogative. It seems a dangerous pastime; my examination of an owl's pellets reveals meals of chipmunk. But life is full of risks,

and there is something to be said for both a good view and a secure territory.

The gray jays move silently through the spruce— almost like gray shadows. I wonder what I could see if I could moved so silently and so freely.

I can see smoke coming from the stove pipe as I enter the meadow, and the two horses set loose to graze spy me and come at a run to get the horse cubes they know I'm carrying in my pocket. I yell out, "Have you got blood on you?" just to let Bill know I'm there. "No, how about you?" comes his answer. "No. Did you see anything? I didn't." "Nope, not a thing." We both lie.

17 October 1991: We are up a full hour and a half before daylight, and breakfast is quickly taken care of. As I am preparing to leave camp I sense that Bill wants to talk, so I don't refuse when he suggests one more cup of coffee. He reminisces about all the years that he has been coming to this camp with his wives and his son. He tells me of the big bull elk and the trophy mule deer he has killed hunting out of this camp, and about the time a bear crashed through his tent, and about the time he found a mule in the camp, and about his years training and breeding fine horses. This almost-monologue goes on for nearly two hours.

Then he announces that this is his last elk hunt, and he asks me if I would spread his ashes here after his death. He points at the slope above camp and says, "Spread them right there where they will go to growing fat deer and elk."

I assure him that I would consider it an honor if that is what he wants. Then it comes to me that he has spent a lot of time on recent trips talking about his last big trout or his last deer hunt or his last time to visit this place or that. It really dawns on me for the first time that Bill is seriously thinking about dying and is getting things—important things to him—settled.

It is settled. He has had his say and he indicates that it is time for me to go hunting. Outside the tent stand the two "camp does" that showed up yesterday. They probably have never seen people before and are quite unafraid. They move off a few yards when I emerge from the tent. I walk slowly across the meadow and start my climb up the mountain. A half hour later I come to a place from where I can look back to camp. Through my binoculars I can see Bill sitting on a stool in the sun feeding salted peanuts to the two deer.

19 October 1991: I am in camp already this evening when Bill returns just at dark. He hunkers near the stove and begins to talk about his last day of elk hunting. A few hours ago he was sitting at the edge of a spruce thicket and built a small fire to make a cup of coffee. He finished the coffee and looked up and saw a perfect five-point bull scenting the smoke and continuing to move toward him. He watched him through his binoculars for several minutes before the bull saw him and disappeared into the trees. "He was so close," Bill says, "that I could see his eyes pop wide open when he saw me.

"That's not a bad ending to your last elk hunt," he continues. "I will always remember that elk when I think of this place. Hell, that elk *is* this place."

14 October 1994: Bill and I arrived at the camp site about an hour before dark. This is one of our favorite camps, with spectacular granite walls surrounding the valley. In quiet moments, the essence of the companions who have camped here with us over the years can be conjured from memory, accompanied by elk and deer hanging from the meat pole, and the ribald jokes, embellished "war stories," serious plans, and—most of all—the comradeship and shared experience that now seem to be eroding slowly away.

16 October 1994: We saw several elk on the morning of the first day, far above us, crossing over the ridge headed for the lower canyon. Besides that one encounter, though, we have seen only one bit of evidence that any elk remain with us in the upper drainage. During this "unsuccessful" hunt, though, we have seen a cougar's track, a marten's track, and mule deer. We have slept in the sun, huddled over small fires to soak up the warmth of the sun stored in the dry wood and released by fire, drunk from running streams, and watched the clouds entangle the summits that surround our valley. We've seen sunrises and sunsets and the moonlight on the gran-

Fog envelops a raghorn bull. (Photo © Henry H. Holdsworth/ Wild by Nature)

ite peaks, and we've heard the wind roar and sigh through the trees. We've eaten well, told lies and jokes, ridden good horses, sipped good bourbon, heard coyotes howl, tramped miles through the snow, been alone and with each other, and have re-created ourselves anew.

23 October 1995: Elk hunting season has arrived at long last—it seems like five years since last year's season—and we have escaped into the wilderness. The horses move quietly along the trail on our way in. Camp is ahead, and that means freedom from the weight they carry, the harness they wear, and a well-earned ration of feed. What else is there—for horses or men? As I watch the sun fade on the mountain peaks, I think to myself that it's an awful long way from Washington, D. C.

The snow at the campsite is about a foot deep; it's a good campsite, sheltered in big spruce trees with flat ground and a plethora of firewood. Unfortunately, Bill is recovering from a serious bout with pneumonia that involved a week in the hospital. He is still a bit on the puny side. That, coupled with his eighty-one years, is a clear indication that the shouldn't be here at 7,000 feet of elevation with a foot of snow. But he knows—and I know—that this is likely his last elk hunt. He wants to be here, puny or not. I believe if he died in his sleeping bag tonight it would be to his liking.

25 October 1995: As we go to bed, sleet begins to drum on the tent fly and seems a lullaby. There is some strange, even smug, satisfaction that comes as you snuggle into a down sleeping bag in a weather-tight tent and imagine the storm outside only inches from your head. But somewhere around midnight a steady pounding rain begins. Heavy rain falling on two feet of snow that rests on frozen ground means that a lot of water will be flowing somewhere, and in very short order. Within minutes the floor of the wall tent is covered with several inches of water.

The immediate job is to get our bedrolls off the tent floor. The second job is to dig a ditch around the tent wall to drain away the water. All hands fall to, and the ditch is complete in about a half hour. The rain stops about an hour later and is replaced by a steady snowfall. We drain a heavy tarpaulin that had been on the tent floor by hanging it from the

ridgepole of the tent along with the sleeping bags. The stove is stuffed with wood and the vent and damper opened wide. When we return to bed, there are no puddles on the damp tarp, and the partially wet sleeping bags are warm. So we sleep wet for the rest of the night, which is not recommended treatment for an eighty-one-year-old man recovering from pneumonia.

Shortly after we bed back down, the camp is wracked by heavy winds, first from downslope and then from upslope. The wind comes with a sound akin to that of an approaching train, and trees crash to the ground around us. It is a night to remember—but not with any fondness.

26 October 1995: Morning finds the sagging tent still erect with the fly intact, but the temperature has dropped to near zero. Bill wakes up complaining that "the air doesn't seem to have much oxygen in it." His breathing is labored, and I offer to ride out with him to the trail head so that he can go home. But, as I expect, he chooses to tough it out. I cook breakfast, then try to put the camp back together in the aftermath of last night's storm. By nine o'clock, all the damp bedrolls are hanging from the roof pole of the tent, damp clothes are hung around the stove, the kitchen gear is all washed and in order, and the stove is chock-full of wood, huffing and puffing and glowing cherry red around the stove pipe. The stove is surrounded by split spruce firewood, and Bill is sitting close to the stove nursing a cup of coffee.

27 October 1995: Bill did not have a good night, and he agrees when pressed that it is time for him to get down the hill and to home. He has made the right decision—though it is a decision that brings him pain. That pain is mostly, I think, bound up in the recognition that he must, finally, make concession to the eighty-one years that he has lived with exuberance. He will not recover from this final recognition. Though he's been saying it for years, this really is his last elk hunt.

By nine o'clock, he and I are off to the trail head with his bedroll and personal gear on one pack horse. We make the trail head by eleven o'clock. Bill is not in good shape, but we conclude that he can get back to town on his own. I watch the truck out of sight down around the first curve, then turn back to load the last hundred pounds of horse feed on the pack horse. It seems a lonely trip back up the trail. It occurs to me that this is the first time in twenty-some-odd years that I look up and don't see Bill at the head of the pack string. In the end, even the toughest and most determined are ground down by the burden of age. Though I am filled with admiration for the long fight and his indomitable spirit, I recognize that his struggle can end in only one way. I hope I can do as well as my time comes.

29 October 1995: It seems strange to saddle the horses and pack up the camp without Bill here singing "Lara's Theme" to the horses, relishing his role as "the packer." Everything goes well, but the day that has been put off—one year at a time—has finally come. Bill is not here.

But, by God, he hung tough to his touchstone as long as physical capability lasted. As I throw the diamond hitch that he carefully taught me, I have a great feeling of loss, of the end of an era. The oldest man still packing these mountains after the snow flies is not here—and likely will not ever be again. Tears run down my cheeks as I tie off the last hitch.

10 October 1996: We have set up in our old elk camp—Bob and Paul and Bill and I. This is, without doubt, my last elk hunting trip into the high Wallowas with my hunting/traveling partner of some twenty-two years. Bill is eighty-two now, and he no longer has the strength to lift a Decker pack saddle onto a horse. He must struggle to get to his feet from a bed on the tent floor. His hands, gnarled with arthritis, hurt too much to deal with the ropes, straps, and buckles of the saddles and packs—particularly when they are frozen by temperatures near zero.

Every year, for at least the last five years, he has proclaimed this or that trip to be his last. This year he said he didn't want to go—and I think he meant it. Bob and Paul and I made it clear that we wanted him to come for no other reason than we wanted his company—and of course only he could handle the string of seven horses. He chose to buy the horse-handling story as the reason to go on this last elk hunt, though he and we all know that I could handle the horses and the packing without trouble. How strange it is that, even among old comrades, there

must be practical excuses for essentially emotional acts. Why could we not say the truth? Why could I not say aloud the words that should be said: "Bill, you are my friend—my real friend—and I love you. I want to be with you in the wilderness one last time. I know you feel the same—just one last time for both our sakes, just one last time."

Why could he not say what he was thinking and feeling? Why could he not say the words that should be said: "Jack, you are my friend and my adopted son. I helped you grow to be what you have become. I showed you the wilderness for the first time. I brought you to see and feel that wilderness. I taught you to pack and to handle a pack string. I showed you your first elk. We have shared much, and I love you. To be with you on my last elk hunt is important to me beyond words. *It must last me for the rest of my life.*"

It is sad that our culture frowns on our saying these things. But somehow I know that those feelings were expressed in code, in ways unspoken.

13 October 1996: Sitting on camp stools in the evening in a wall tent with snow pouring down and stew bubbling on the stove is an experience to be savored in the present as well as in memory. As the snow accumulates on the tent fly, it is necessary to "beat off the snow" occasionally by striking the top of the tent with the back of the hand—otherwise there is real danger of the tent's collapsing. Bill allows that the only thing he's found at all useful about having an enlarged prostate and drinking alcohol before bedtime is that you have to get up frequently during the night to beat the snow off the tent and put more wood in the stove.

Now that's putting a positive spin on things.

Bob and Paul find no fresh elk sign on this day. Bill and I stay in camp and talk away the day—mostly he talks and I listen. He needs to talk—of other hunts, of other days—and to tell me the old stories just one last time. He is saying goodbye.

The softly falling snow comes all day, muffling sound so completely that, in the short lulls in conversation, we can hear our own breathing and even the pulse in our ears. Even in the silence, though, we are aware of each other's presence and of the quality of this time that will not come again. We have ridden thousands of miles together, camped together

Above: *Without question, the bull elk is the king of North American big game. (Photo © John W. Herbst)*
Right: *Water and plenty of forage satisfy this bull. (Photo © Sherm Spoelstra)*

for hundreds of nights, and have shared the wilderness and each other's company. I think this is the last time, and so does Bill.

He says it is time to move from his farm in the foothills into town. But how will he live without his horses, without hunting and fishing, without pheasants and bird dogs? How will he make it without these trips to the wilderness?

He will bear the curse of a life that goes on when the gusto and the joy and the challenge have faded to nothing.

In the afternoon, I take my hunting pack and walk up the mountain behind camp until I am at tree line. As I look across at the granite wall that towers above camp, I remember the first time I rode into this valley some twenty or so years ago. I think now exactly what sprang to mind then. "Where were you Job, when I laid down the pillars of the earth?"

And then I know that I will not come here again. It would not be the same without Bill. To come here alone, or with others, would diminish the spirit of the place and the treasured memories that reside here. It will be better, I think, to lock the essence of the place and time in my mind and not return except in reverie.

This is a trip of endings. My career in the Forest Service is at an end. Bill's "oneness" with his wilderness is coming to a close. But there are no endings without simultaneous beginnings. The sadness and sense of loss that wash over me alternate with relief, and eagerness to begin anew, and the knowledge that other places and other times will be as good, or even better, than these.

Then there is a movement far below and just out from the tent. Through my binoculars I can see that Bill has taken a camp stool and walked out in the open and is seated looking up toward the granite walls. He sits there in the sun for over an hour, almost without movement.

Epilogue, Fall 1997: Bill and I have sold our horses and most of our equipment. I have retired as chief of the Forest Service, and now teach school to budding young biologists. I look into young faces and try to see another Bill Brown aborning. That is in vain, I suspect—maybe there are some that are simply one of a kind.

Bob Nelson has retired as well. Randy Fisher has moved on to other things. We will never be together again in the high lonesome except in reverie—but a part of each of us is there forever. Perhaps that essence combines with the elk that are there to become the spirit of a special place. At least it does in my mind.

I think the philospher Ortega y Gassett spoke truth when he said something to the effect that true hunters do not hunt in order to kill. Rather, they kill in order to have hunted. And so it was with us.

HUNTING HONEYMOON

By Patricia Simpson

Patricia Simpson is a freelance writer living in the Pacific Northwest. Her beautiful surroundings in the foothills of the Cascades include a herd of twenty-five elk, which routinely make themselves at home in her backyard. This piece originally appeared in *Sports Afield.*

Simpson's elk camp verifies that elk hunts come in all shapes and sizes. Having never hunted before, Simpson met the love of her life and, after an extended courtship, decided to tie the knot. Her new husband loved to hunt. So what better way to celebrate than to go hunting for wapiti? Ladies and gentleman: Elk camp as honeymoon suite.

Weddings are so romantic: the bride in her long dress, the groom handsome in his tuxedo. And then there's that special moment when the happy couple change into long underwear and wool clothes, climb into their 4WD and go elk hunting.

Perhaps I should go back to the beginning and explain. Norm asked me to marry him in February. We were camped on the beach in a snowstorm. (This should have been my first clue.) I couldn't wait to get home and tell my mother. She'd be so glad we were finally tying the knot.

I called her when we returned. "Hi, Mom. Norm and I are getting married."

"Thank goodness! When?"

"Sometime this fall. We can't set the date until June."

I hoped that by saying this with great assurance I could get by with no further questions. I should have known better.

"Why June? What's the problem?" My mother was getting suspicious. She could always tell when I was fudging the truth.

"The game laws won't be out till then," I explained to her.

"What do the game laws have to do with your wedding?"

"We are going elk hunting on our honeymoon, and we can't set the date until we know when the season opens."

There was dead silence on the other end of the phone. I thought my mother was in shock. Well, she'd get over this trauma before too long.

"Weddings are so romantic: the bride in her long dress, the groom handsome in his tuxedo. And there's that special moment when the happy couple change into long underwear and wool clothes, climb into their 4WD and go elk hunting." —Patricia Simpson (Photo © Jeffrey Rich)

We take care of all the important paperwork next. We get our marriage license. I buy my first hunting license. I also apply for something called a "controlled hunt permit." As I understand it, this will allow me to shoot any elk I see, bull or cow. I think it is real nice when my name is drawn and I receive this permit. After all, how many states would make it so easy for a beginning hunter? Norm goes off muttering something about "dumb luck." Seems he's never gotten one of these permits. Maybe they didn't have them when he was a beginner.

Shopping for my trousseau was interesting. I don't think I'll ever forget the look on the saleslady's face when I told her that I was buying that heavy flannel plaid nightshirt for my wedding night. She obviously didn't spend *her* honeymoon in the woods.

We were married at my sister's house on November 1. It was a Saturday that year. Elk season began on Monday. After all the toasts and gift-opening, we left and drove home. We picked up the Jeep and the camper, packed our clothes and headed for the hills.

We spent our wedding night in a roadside rest area. We had started out later than we had planned and couldn't make our destination. We had the whole place to ourselves, except for six or seven semis. Diesel fumes are so alluring. We set out again the next morning and soon reached our campsite. The sun was shining, a light breeze was blowing, the temperature was about 65° F. I thought it was great. Norm, however, was not pleased. Evidently this was not the kind of weather you want for elk hunting.

Since the conditions stayed that way for the entire first week of the season, I will not dwell on our hunting success. We walked for miles and never saw a thing except chipmunks, and they weren't in season.

It was a wonderful first week of marriage, though. I cooked gourmet dinners of hamburger and fried potatoes on the two-burner stove. We ate by the glow of a hissing gas lantern. We played passionate games of gin rummy with the hunters from the next camp. I understand poker is the usual game in elk camps, but after I cleaned them all out at

Cows and calves up with the sun. (Photo © Henry H. Holdsworth/Wild by Nature)

An elk calf tip-toes across Wyoming's Madison River. (Photo © Barbara von Hoffmann)

five-card stud, they started muttering about "dumb luck" again and wouldn't play with me anymore. (I had a very enlightened childhood. My cousins taught me poker before I could walk.)

The second week started with a blizzard. The temperature dropped close to zero and several feet of snow fell in the next day and a half. This seemed to me like the perfect time to go home, before we got snowed in and ended up spending our first anniversary on the mountain.

Norm was now happy. This was just what was needed to get those elk moving. If I had been those elk, I would have been moving too—to somewhere like California, where it was warm.

So it was decided. The snow had stopped. We would start our hunt bright and early the next morning. It was so early in fact that it was too dark to see if it was bright. I bundled into my down parka and bravely set out behind Norm.

* * *

Several days later we arrived at the chosen stand. (Norm says it was only an hour or so, but I know better.) We settled down against a rock to wait for daylight. It eventually caught up with us and tried to pretend it had been there all the time. Spread out below our rock was a narrow valley. Norm felt sure that sometime during the morning an elk was going to cross that valley and become locker meat. Since I knew almost nothing about elk, I was willing to trust him.

This touching trust lasted about three hours. At that point I stood up to stretch and discovered that a dozen elk had tiptoed across the clearing behind our rock and disappeared into the valley behind us. There were tracks everywhere! We returned to camp to thaw out and regroup. This was only a minor setback.

After lunch we set out in a different direction. This time we were walking a small ridge between two prairies. Elk had been seen feeding there before.

A light breeze of about 30 mph had sprung up

A bull elk on a ridgeline. (Photo © Michael H. Francis)

and I was slowly starting to freeze. In order to stuff my cold hands into my warm pockets, I had to sling my gun across my back. (Okay, so I'm not a great white hunter.) Norm was about 20 yards in front of me.

When I lifted my head to follow him, I found myself staring into the eyes of a very large cow elk. She was also about 20 yards away, but off to one side. Now I was in a fix. I couldn't move, I couldn't shoot, and Norm was looking the other way.

I was standing there in total confusion when Norm turned around to see where I was. Just then the elk leaped in midair, did a 180-degree turn and disappeared.

Norm's reaction was immediate. "How long had that (¢$%@ elk been there?"

"About a minute," I replied. "I couldn't shoot, I couldn't get to my gun."

There was silence as he realized where the gun was. I thought the honeymoon was over.

The next morning we get into the Jeep and head for a distant meadow. Norm has forgiven me. Today we will sit in the relative comfort of the Jeep and watch for elk.

Several hours later I happened to glance over my shoulder at a clearing behind us and spotted five grazing elk. I nudged Norm. He quietly slid off his seat, keeping the Jeep between him and the elk. Using the vehicle as a steady rest, he fired.

Nothing happened. He fired again. The elk looked around and went back to eating. He fired a third shot. The largest elk jerked as if he'd been hit, and they all thundered out of sight. Upon closer inspection we found there was no blood, just three clean misses. This was going to be a long day.

The next morning it snowed heavily and we were stuck in camp. Norm paced back and forth in our 10-foot camper. I devised 47 different ways to cheat at solitaire. Something had to come out right. The hours passed slowly.

When the next day dawns, our enthusiasm is at a low ebb. I am firmly convinced that there are no

elk out there with our name on them. The trip is jinxed, and worse, it's a failure. Norm's expression reveals thoughts only a shade more cheerful than mine. We fool around in camp until well past daylight.

We reluctantly dragged our feet out of camp and decided to go back to our original stand. Soon there was a herd of elk standing below us in that narrow valley. Actually, there were only four of them. But the way this trip had been going, that's a lot.

So I shot one. Hey, this isn't so hard! My elk tag is now filled. It's only a cow, but it's my first elk. We have meat in camp and the trip is successful.

The dictionary defines a honeymoon as "a period of harmony immediately following marriage." Under that definition, our honeymoon lasted two days. After that, the difficulties of life in a small camper got in the way.

I have to admit that this was not your usual honeymoon. I don't even think it was a good example of an elk trip. In fact, after nine seasons of celebrating our anniversary in one elk camp or another, I know it wasn't. But we must have done something right. We keep going back to relive our hunting honeymoon.

A Roosevelt elk silhouetted against the Pacific Ocean. (Photo © Jeffrey Rich)

Chapter 5

REACHING THE PINNACLE OF BIG GAME HUNTING

"If the truth be known, elk hunting is a tough, sweaty business, conducted at breathtaking elevations among blowdowns too low to crawl under and too high to step over. Along with the cash cost, you'll pay for your animal in sore muscles, starved lungs, and time."
—Norman Strung, Field & Stream, 1976

DAVID'S MOUNTAIN

by Eileen Clarke

Successfully hunting elk is, to many hunters, the very pinnacle of big game hunting. The regal elk is that grand, that majestic. And the challenge of chasing wapiti across the snowy mountains of the West will test the stamina of the heartiest of hunters.

Eileen Clarke has been there, and she knows well the tenacity required to bring an elk home. Eileen is the cooking columnist for *Field & Stream* magazine and the author of several books, including *The Art of Wild Game Cooking*, *The Venison Cookbook*, and a novel, *The Queen of the Legal Tender Saloon*. Her writing has also appeared in *Gray's Sporting Journal*, *Wyoming Wildlife*, and *Shooting Sportsman*. She grew up in New York City, but now makes her home in Montana—elk country.

David's Mountain had elk. They were not mythical or illusory or non-existent. David watched them in the spring from the seat of his ancient John Deere tractor as he planted wheat, and in the hot baked afternoons of July, trying to get his hay crop in before the elk ate, bedded, and trampled the profits out of it. By late August after the spring wheat was harvested, he would call on his friends up and down the canyon to make sure they would come and hunt elk on his land each fall. But David hadn't hunted elk in twenty-five years. He'd forgotten how fast elk disappear when you turn the tractor broadside and cut the engine.

My husband John and I were among those friends David invited to hunt. We began stalking them with bow and arrow, diaphragm and grunt tube in early September. We called one bull in only to have the wind switch on us as the six-point elk headed nose-first up the mountain at us. As soon as the wind swirled from the back of my neck to his nose, he wheeled. Bolting through the herd, he pulled those cows, calves, and satellite bulls behind him tight as a hundred-car train.

One day in early October, we stood in camouflaged ambush halfway up the first big ridge, waiting for the herd to finish feeding in David's alfalfa field and head uphill to its bedding ground. But another hunter slipped in behind us. He dropped his cow call and, just as the herd came to him, started rooting around in the brush for it. The herd came up the paths they always used and past our stands, but they came through at eighty miles an hour,

Pages 118–119: *"Oh, the days of elk and buffalo! / It fills my heart with pain / To know these days are past and gone / To never come again."—Traditional Western Ballad (Photo © Henry H. Holdsworth/Wild by Nature)*

Page 119, inset: *Two hunters pose with an elk shot in the Cypress Hills area of Saskatchewan, 1956. (Photo courtesy Saskatchewan Archives Board)*

Opposite: *The mystique of elk places them squarely at the pinnacle of big game hunting. (Photo © Stan Osolinski/ The Green Agency)*

nostrils flared, and heads held high like parched camels sniffing out water.

The hunter followed shortly after, mumbling about his lost call and how much it cost him. He asked me where I thought the elk might go, insisting that he could catch up with them before nightfall. John and I packed up our gear and headed back downhill to regroup.

In late October, we headed out again. This time, we carried rifles, expanding our effective range by 250 yards. We drove past the spots David and his friends had named over the past thirty years while they killed elk off the mountain—the loose gate, the Scenic Route, David's Old Sawmill, The Hole, Tree Stands Number Two, Three and Four, then got out and walked uphill past the Rock Pile, Big Tree Hole, and halfway to Priscilla's Knob.

The first day of rifle season we saw legs. Criss-crossed, gangly teenage-girl legs danced beneath an enormous pine log that lay in the middle of a ten-acre blow-down. There was no way we could go under, over, or around without twisting a knee, spraining an ankle, and alarming the entire wildlife population of David's mountain.

One other day, we saw ears—sixteen of them—belonging to four cows and four calves, bouncing up and down on the far side of a snowy side ridge. We waited, hoping for a set of antlers, but none appeared. On David's mountain, in rifle season, that meant no legal elk.

November began with a freeze and thaw, freeze and thaw; then snow, and another freeze and thaw. We hunted one morning along the creek bottom—during the second freeze—thinking the elk would try to stay at lower, somewhat warmer elevations, too. John and I wore so many layers of wool, Thinsulate, and polypropylene we looked like Pillsbury dough-people. And, for a while, we stayed relatively comfortable.

We set up stands three hundred yards apart along the last row of trees beside the creek. I heard elk. Or at least I heard something in the brush wheezing. I saw two ducks floating in a little eddy in the creek, preening and feeding like it was a midsummer's afternoon. That only made me colder. And the colder I got, the harder it was to concentrate on elk.

A cow and calf cross the Yellowstone River. (Photo © Jeff and Alexa Henry)

I stuck till the sun rose, then waited for the sun to appear over the top of the mountain. In the course of that first half hour of light, I discovered a fact Paleolothic man probably learned the first time he tried to ambush a wooly mammoth: When the sun comes up, it gets colder before it gets warmer. A lot colder. Or maybe it's just that you let your guard down. Just when you think the sun's going to save your bacon, your fingers and toes are no longer quietly numb—they've begun to throb and burn. It's a symptom, like when the snowbank starts to look cozy and warm.

I quickly gathered my pack and thermal seat and walked as competently as my frozen legs allowed back toward the dirt road. And as I clumsily removed the magazine from my rifle to cross the barbed wire fence, I realized another important fact: I was as tough as my husband John. Three hundred yards down the barbed wire fence, he was removing the magazine from his rifle and doing it just as clumsily as I had.

The next week, it snowed and thawed, then froze and snowed and thawed. We went out again during the second thaw thinking the elk might be moving around in the sixty-five-degree afternoons eating the newly cleared grass and trying to find drier beds. Good theory. We actually saw elk. They were 1000 yards below us, walking across a Forest Service road. Then we saw two guys in a pickup dressed head to toe in hunter's orange shoot into the herd and miss. The elk ran into the next state. We walked back to our truck, trying to keep to the high ground, but ended up completely encased in an inch of mud. So much for balmy weather elk hunting.

By the last week of November, we'd spent twenty-seven days hunting elk. Not only didn't we have an elk, we had gotten so caught up in our quest we had added no other meat to the freezer either. We had some antelope and venison left over from the previous year, but we needed at least one deer this year. Whitetail, muley, doe, or buck. That would get us to the next season when we would be more moderate in our goals.

Then David came to visit.

"There's elk all over the mountain," he said. "You guys gotta help me thin 'em out. You should see what they do to my alfalfa fields."

He'd brought along his little blue-and-white cooler which held a six-pack of Lucky Lager. He took the second beer out. David was Old World, son of Polish immigrants and a Depression era baby besides: He never wanted to impose. So the cooler of beer went with him whenever he visited his friends up the canyon.

He twisted our arms further. "They say elk is the best tasting meat you can cook. And it's low in cholesterol, which is something to think about, you know." He'd had triple bypass surgery two years before. "Lots of things you got to think about."

"But, David," I said. "We've spent all season on this elk chase. I need to put a little meat in the freezer. We've got to do a little deer hunting."

"You still got a week," he said, popping open a third can of beer. "You hunt elk 'til Friday. Then you got lots of time to get venison."

He pronounced "venison" the way a cattleman would say "tofu."

"We can just buy a few more bags of beans and rice," I suggested to John. "We've tried this hard. It's kinda a shame to give up so soon."

David nodded at him. "Lots of meat. Good meat. It's like the ladies, John. There's no such thing as bad elk."

John laughed. "Fine by me," he said. "I've always had a hard time saying 'no' to a rancher who begs."

"Good," David said, toasting John with his Lucky Lager. "Tomorrow morning."

"When the going gets tough, the tough go elk hunting," David said and returned his empty to the cooler, popping open another can.

But hard as we tried, we found no legal elk on the mountain those next four days. Cows and calves by the dozens, but the innocent spikes had already been harvested and the big bulls had retreated to their secret spots to wait out the last week of hunting season.

Friday night came. Only two mornings left to hunt. We spent the evening plotting out strategy and came up with a modest approach. With the help of some friends who also needed some meat, we would spend the next two mornings conducting a whitetail drive. The first morning on the south side of the creek that ran along the bottom of David's mountain, and the second north of the creek in the thick aspen-and-bramble coulee just at the base of the mountain.

Pursuing elk means you've got to go up—to the mountains. (Photo © Michael Mauro)

The south side produced one fat whitetail doe—amidst a lot of whooping and coughing and cursing over twisted ankles—with a good shot by a man with nothing in his freezer, so he took the whole animal home.

On the last day, Sunday, five of us remained: John and I, our friends Norm and Sil, and Sil's brother Iron Mike. We arrived at the base of the coulee just before dawn, climbed out of the trucks and buttoned up quickly and tightly against the fourteen-below chill. We would warm up halfway up the mountain. 'Til then, it was a holding action, keeping the warm kitchen air trapped inside our clothes.

The plan was for the three men to walk halfway up the first ridge before shooting light and sit above the first grove of aspen. Then, at legal light, Sil and I would start working our way slowly up the ridge through the thick brush, pausing every now and then and staring all around us trying to make the deer think they'd been spotted.

Forty-five minutes later, I was just below where John, Norm, and Iron Mike were waiting, only twenty yards inside the edge of alders. I heard a shot. I listened for more, but there was only the one.

"Good," I thought to myself. One shot in this crowd usually meant a clean kill. Two was bad, unless there was a very long pause. Three, forget it. You were back at square one.

I cleared the top of the aspen, and walked up to where John was sitting. While I caught my breath, I started pulling sticky seeds off my wool jacket and pants.

"I heard a shot," I said. "What happened?"

"I don't know," he said. "Wasn't us."

Then we heard two shots, and two more, and Norm, who was sitting higher on the hillside, waved us down and quiet, pointing toward the top of the coulee on our right.

One more rifle shot came from that direction, then the sound of a herd running, growing louder.

"Get ready," Norm whispered. "Elk, and I see one set of legal horns."

Before Norm finished his sentence, the first cows and calves came over the hill at a gallop, followed by sixty more.

The four of us scanned the top of the herd looking for antlers. Ears, ears, ears, and ears. And just as

suddenly as the elk appeared they were about to disappear into the aspen grove.

"Where's Sil?" I whispered.

John shrugged his shoulders, concentrating on the herd below us.

The lead cow suddenly pulled up. She turned back from the aspens, looking toward the top of the coulee she'd just run from. She hadn't seen us; I knew that. Then as the herd circled slowly and indecisively above the trees, I realized it had to be Sil holding them. She was still only halfway up the ridge, standing in the middle of the only cover the elk could reach quickly. The herd grew more nervous, pacing with their noses high, sniffing the air, ready to bolt as soon as any one of them decided which way was safe.

All this time I'd been searching through my four-power scope, trying to find the spike. "There he is," I whispered to myself.

John looked down where my rifle was pointed.

"Twenty feet from the edge of the aspen," I said. "But there's a cow in front of him."

"Soon as he's clear."

"Now he's facing away."

"Soon as he's broadside."

Broadside. He turned broadside almost before John said it and I shot. The herd blew past the spike and back up over the ridge, leaving the spike standing flat-footed, head down, unaware that he was the only elk on the mountain.

I lined up the crosshairs on his chest again and fired, but the spike collapsed before the bullet reached him.

"Good job," John said, whacking me on the back. I still hadn't spotted him. He gave me a hand up.

"Legs are shaking," I said, grinning.

Norm walked up to us and unloaded his gun. "Well, guys, I don't know about you, but I don't think we can do anything to top this. I think we should declare hunting season over, and after we go say good morning to Uncle David, we should park ourselves in front of a good football game."

David was full of "I told you so's" as we warmed up around his fire.

"Now where did you get him?" he asked.

"Right above the creek. Half a mile up the Scenic Route," I told him.

"Now what did I tell you? They're all over the

Above: *Stopping for a cool drink along a Colorado stream. (Photo © Michael Mauro)*
Overleaf: *Elk and bighorn sheep occasionally cross paths in their mountainous homes. (Photo © Sherm Spoelstra)*

mountain. They're easy. I don't know what you make such a fuss about. I feel like I'm running cattle sometimes. Feed 'em and water 'em."

"Yes, David," I said. "Thank you for letting me hunt your mountain."

"Oh, you bet. Maybe next year you and John both get one, now you get the hang of it."

We all shuffled toward the door, coats open, boots unlaced, warm from the fire and David's coffee, looking forward to a day indoors with our feet up in front of the T.V.

David started to walk us out to the trucks. "You wouldn't be interested in a few geese would you?" he asked. "There's still a month of goose season, I think. I got lots of geese coming in, eating on my winter wheat sprouts. Making a mess of the field. You know they're really good to eat and good for you. Not like that chicken you buy at the store. You know commercial chicken just doesn't have any flavor anymore. Tastes like cardboard. Or oatmeal. . . ."

Norm signalled for everyone to load up in the trucks. Football games were starting. "Come on down for cocktails tonight, David," he said.

"Oh, no, Norm; I couldn't do that."

"Bring your cooler," Norm suggested.

"Well, maybe for a little while. We can talk about the geese," he suggested. "You know, those geese grow better when they get thinned out a little. There's nothing to it."

Chapter 6

---❖---

MAJESTIC
ELK

*"The moose is larger, the grizzly bear more powerful, the mountain lion
more mysterious, and the whitetail more graceful, but the bull wapiti, with
his proud posture, bugled call to arms, and rich, tricolored pelage . . . is
certainly the most regal of North America's wild creatures."*
— David Petersen, Among the Elk, 1988

THE WAPITI OR ROUND-HORNED ELK

By Theodore Roosevelt

Before Theodore Roosevelt ever rode with the Rough Riders, entered the White House after the assassination of William McKinley, acquired the Panama Canal Zone, or won the Nobel Peace Prize, he hunted elk. He took a strong interest in the natural world at an early age, and entertained thoughts of becoming a naturalist up until his college years.

Despite his eastern upbringing, having been born in New York City and educated at Harvard, Roosevelt was drawn west. In 1883, at the tender age of twenty-four, Roosevelt acquired two ranches in the Dakota Territory—Chimney Butte and Elkhorn, the latter name due to discovering interlocked elk antlers at the site of the ranch.

Though Roosevelt only stayed in the Dakota Territory until 1886, returning to New York at that time to pursue his political ambitions, the Wild West had a profound effect on him. His literary output during this period is remarkable. In addition to titles you might expect of a politician with national aspirations, such as *The Naval War of 1812* and *The Winning of the West*, Roosevelt penned reminiscences of his life in the West. These included *Hunting Trips of a Ranchman* and *The Wilderness Hunter*, from which this excerpt was taken.

Once while on another hunt with John Willis, I spent a week in a vain effort to kill moose among the outlying mountains at the southern end of the Bitter Root range. Then, as we had no meat, we determined to try for elk, of which we had seen much sign.

We were camped with a wagon, as high among the foot-hills as wheels could go, but several hours' walk from the range of the game; for it was still early in the season, and they had not yet come down from the upper slopes. Accordingly we made a practice of leaving the wagon for two or three days at a time to hunt; returning to get a night's rest in the tent, preparatory to a fresh start. On these trips we carried neither blankets nor packs, as the

Pages 130–131: *From their winsome bugle to their lordly bearing, there can be no doubt that the elk is majesty found. (Photo © Michael Mauro)*
Page 131, inset: *A bull elk on the Flathead–Couer d'Alene Reservation, circa 1940. (Courtesy of the Museum of New Mexico, Neg. Number 112879)*
Opposite: *Even in Roosevelt's day, the majestic elk had already retreated to North America's remotest wildernesses. (Photo © Michael Mauro)*

walking was difficult and we had much ground to cover. Each merely put on his jacket with a loaf of frying-pan bread and a paper of salt stuffed into the pockets. We were cumbered with nothing save our rifles and cartridges.

On the morning in question we left camp at sunrise. For two or three hours we walked up-hill through a rather open growth of small pines and spruces, the travelling being easy. Then we came to the edge of a deep valley, a couple of miles across. Into this we scrambled, down a steep slide, where the forest had grown up among the immense boulder masses. The going here was difficult to a degree; the great rocks, dead timber, slippery pine needles, and loose gravel entailing caution at every step, while we had to guard our rifles carefully from the consequences of a slip. It was not much better at the bottom, which was covered by a tangled mass of swampy forest. Through this we hunted carefully, but with no success, in spite of our toil; for the only tracks we saw that were at all fresh were those of a cow and calf moose. Finally, in the afternoon, we left the valley and began to climb a steep gorge, down which a mountain torrent roared and foamed in a succession of cataracts.

Three hours' hard climbing brought us to another valley, but of an entirely different character. It was several miles long, but less than a mile broad. Save at the mouth, it was walled in completely by chains of high rock-peaks, their summits snow-capped; the forest extended a short distance up their sides. The bottom of the valley was in places covered by open woodland, elsewhere by marshy meadows, dotted with dense groves of spruce.

Hardly had we entered this valley before we caught a glimpse of a yearling elk walking rapidly along a game path some distance ahead. We followed as quickly we could without making a noise, but after the first glimpse never saw it again; for it is astonishing how fast an elk travels, with its ground-covering walk.

Right: *With plenty of immature pines to snack on, two bulls dawdle in the safety of a burned-out forest. (Photo © Stan Osolinski/The Green Agency)*
Overleaf: *The beauty of a bull elk is enhanced that much more by the beauty of his habitat. (Photo © Jeff Foott)*

We went up the valley until we were well past its middle, and saw abundance of fresh elk sign. Evidently two or three bands had made the neighborhood their headquarters. Among them were some large bulls, which had been trying their horns not only on the quaking-asp and willow saplings, but also on one another, though the rut had barely begun. By one pool they had scooped out a kind of wallow or bare spot in the grass, and had torn and tramped the ground with their hoofs. The place smelt strongly of their urine.

By the time the sun set we were sure the elk were towards the head of the valley. We utilized the short twilight in arranging our sleeping place for the night, choosing a thick grove of spruce beside a small mountain tarn, at the foot of a great cliff. We were chiefly influenced in our choice by the abundance of dead timber of a size easy to handle; the fuel question being all-important on such a trip, where one has to lie out without bedding, and to keep up a fire, with no axe to cut wood.

Having selected a smooth spot, where some low-growing firs made a wind break, we dragged up enough logs to feed the fire throughout the night. Then we drank our fill at the icy pool, and ate a few mouthfuls of bread. While it was still light we heard the querulous bleat of the conies, from among the slide rocks at the foot of the mountain; and the chipmunks and chickarees scolded at us. As dark came on, and we sat silently gazing into the flickering blaze, the owls began muttering and hooting.

Clearing the ground of stones and sticks, we lay down beside the fire, pulled our soft felt hats over our ears, buttoned our jackets, and went to sleep. Of course our slumbers were fitful and broken, for every hour or two the fire got low and had to be replenished. We wakened shivering out of each spell of restless sleep to find the logs smouldering; we were alternately scorched and frozen.

As the first faint streak of dawn appeared in the dark sky my companion touched me lightly on the arm. The fire was nearly out; we felt numbed by the chill air. At once we sprang up, stretched our arms, shook ourselves, examined our rifles, swallowed a mouthful or two of bread, and walked off through the gloomy forest.

At first we could scarcely see our way, but it grew rapidly lighter. The gray mist rose and wavered over the pools and wet places; the morning voices of the wilderness began to break the death-like stillness. After we had walked a couple of miles the mountain tops on our right hand reddened in the sun-rays.

Then, as we trod noiselessly over the dense moss, and on the pine needles under the scattered trees, we heard a sharp clang and clatter up the valley ahead of us. We knew this meant game of some sort; and stealing lightly and cautiously forward we soon saw before us the cause of the noise.

In a little glade, a hundred and twenty-five yards from us, two bull elk were engaged in deadly combat, while two others were looking on. It was a splendid sight. The great beasts faced each other with lowered horns, the manes that covered their thick necks, and the hair on their shoulders, bristling and erect. Then they charged furiously, the crash of the meeting antlers resounding through the valley. The shock threw them both on their haunches, with locked horns and glaring eyes they strove against each other, getting their hind legs well under them, straining every muscle in their huge bodies, and squealing savagely. They were evenly matched in weight, strength, and courage; and push as they might, neither got the upper hand, first one yielding a few inches, then the other, while they swayed to and fro in their struggles, smashing the bushes and ploughing up the soil.

Finally they separated and stood some little distance apart, under the great pines; their sides heaving, and columns of steam rising from their nostrils through the frosty air of the brightening morning. Again they rushed with a crash, and each strove mightily to overthrow the other, or get past his guard; but the branching antlers caught every vicious lunge and thrust. This set-to was stopped rather curiously. One of the onlooking elk was a yearling; the other, though scarcely as heavy-bodied

Opposite, top: *"The great beasts faced each other with lowered horns, the manes that covered their thick necks, and the hair on their shoulders, bristling and erect. Then they charged furiously, the crash of the meeting antlers resounding through the valley."*—Theodore Roosevelt *(Photo © Jeff Foott)*

Opposite, bottom: *It is late spring in the Rocky Mountains and a calf turns to its mother for sustenance. (Photo © Jeff Foott)*

A velvety elk forages on a lush summer hillside. (Photo © Jeff and Alexa Henry)

as either of the fighters, had a finer head. He was evidently much excited by the battle, and he now began to walk towards the two combatants, nodding his head and uttering a queer, whistling noise. They dared not leave their flanks uncovered to his assault; and as he approached they promptly separated, and walked off side by side a few yards apart. In a moment, however, one spun round and jumped at his old adversary, seeking to stab him in his unprotected flank; but the latter was just as quick, and as before caught the rush on his horns. They closed as furiously as ever; but the utmost either could do was to inflict one or two punches on the neck and shoulders of his foe, where the thick hide served as a shield. Again the peace-maker approached, nodding

his head, whistling, and threatening; and again they separated.

This was repeated once or twice; and I began to be afraid lest the breeze which was very light and puffy should shift and give them my wind. So, resting my rifle on my knee I fired twice, putting one bullet behind the shoulder of the peace-maker, and the other behind the shoulder of one of the combatants. Both were deadly shots, but, as so often with wapiti, neither of the wounded animals at the moment showed any signs of being hit. The yearling ran off unscathed. The other three crowded together and trotted behind some spruce on the left, while we ran forward for another shot. In a moment one fell; whereupon the remaining two turned and came back across the glade, trotting to the right. As we opened fire they broke into a lumbering gallop, but were both downed before they got out of sight in the timber.

As soon as the three bulls were down we busied ourselves taking off their heads and hides, and cutting off the best portions of the meat—from the saddles and hams—to take back to camp, where we smoked it. But first we had breakfast. We kindled a fire beside a little spring of clear water and raked out the coals. Then we cut two willow twigs as spits, ran on each a number of small pieces of elk loin, and roasted them over the fire. We had salt; we were very hungry; and I never ate anything that tasted better. The wapiti is, next to the moose, the most quarrelsome and pugnacious of American deer. It cannot be said that it is ordinarily a dangerous beast to hunt; yet there are instances in which wounded wapiti, incautiously approached to within striking distance, have severely misused their assailants, both with their antlers and their forefeet. I myself knew one man who had been badly mauled in this fashion. When tamed the bulls are dangerous to human life in the rutting season. In a grapple they are of course infinitely more to be dreaded than ordinary deer, because of their great strength.

However, the fiercest wapiti bull, when in a wild state, flees the neighborhood of man with the same panic terror shown by the cows; and he makes no stand against a grisly, though when his horns are grown he has little fear of either wolf or cougar if on his guard and attacked fairly. The chief battles of the bulls are of course waged with one another. Before the beginning of the rut they keep by themselves: singly, while the sprouting horns are still very young, at which time they lie in secluded spots and move about as little as possible; in large bands, later in the season. At the beginning of the fall these bands join with one another and with the bands of cows and calves, which have likewise been keeping to themselves during the late winter, the spring, and the summer. Vast herds are thus sometimes formed, containing, in the old days when wapiti were plenty, thousands of head. The bulls now begin to fight furiously with one another, and the great herd becomes split into smaller ones. Each of these has one master bull, who has won his position by savage battle and keeps it by overcoming every rival, whether

a solitary bull, or the lord of another harem, who challenges him. When not fighting or love-making he is kept on the run, chasing away the young bulls who venture to pay court to the cows. He has hardly time to eat or sleep, and soon becomes gaunt and worn to a degree. At the close of the rut many of the bulls become so emaciated that they retire to some secluded spot to recuperate. They are so weak that they readily succumb to the elements, or to their brute foes; many die from sheer exhaustion.

The battles between the bulls rarely result fatally. After a longer or shorter period of charging, pushing, and struggling the heavier or more enduring of the two begins to shove his weaker antagonist back and round; and the latter then watches his chance and bolts, hotly, but as a rule harmlessly, pursued for a few hundred yards. The massive branching antlers serve as effective guards against the most wicked thrusts. While the antagonists are head on, the worst that can happen is a punch on the shoulder which will not break the thick hide, though it may bruise the flesh underneath. It is only when a beast is caught while turning that there is a chance to deliver a possibly deadly stab in the flank, with the brow prongs, the "dogkillers" as they are called in bucks. Sometimes, but rarely, fighting wapiti get their antlers interlocked and perish miserably; my own ranch, the Elkhorn, was named from finding on the spot where the ranch house now stands two splendid pairs of elk antlers thus interlocked. . . .

During the rut the bulls are very noisy; and their notes of amorous challenge are called "whistling" by the frontiersmen,—very inappropriately. They begin to whistle about ten days before they begin to run; and they have in addition an odd kind of bark, which is only heard occasionally. The whistling is a most curious, and to me a most attractive sound, when heard in the great lonely mountains. As with so many other things, much depends upon the surroundings. When listened to nearby and under unfavorable circumstances, the sound resembles a succession of hoarse whistling roars, ending with two or three gasping grunts.

But heard at a little distance, and in its proper place, the call of the wapiti is one of the grandest and most beautiful sounds in nature. Especially is this the case when several rivals are answering one another, on some frosty moonlight night in the mountains. The wild melody rings from chasm to chasm under the giant pines, sustained and modulated, through bar after bar, filled with challenge and proud anger. It thrills the soul of the listening hunter.

Once, while in the mountains, I listened to a peculiarly grand chorus of this kind. We were travelling with pack ponies at the time, and our tent was pitched in a grove of yellow pine, by a brook in the bottom of a valley. On either hand rose the mountains, covered with spruce forest. It was in September, and the first snow had just fallen.

The day before we had walked long and hard; and during the night I slept the heavy sleep of the weary. Early in the morning, just as the east began to grow gray, I waked; and as I did so, the sounds that smote on my ear, caused me to sit up and throw off the warm blankets. Bull elk were challenging among the mountains on both sides of the valley, a little way from us, their notes echoing like the calling of silver bugles. Groping about in the dark, I drew on my trousers, an extra pair of thick socks, and my moccasins, donned a warm jacket, found my fur cap and gloves, and stole out of the tent with my rifle.

The air was very cold; the stars were beginning to pale in the dawn; on the ground the snow glimmered white, and lay in feathery masses on the branches of the balsams and young pines. The air rang with the challenges of many wapiti; their incessant calling came pealing down through the still, snow-laden woods. First one bull challenged; then another answered; then another and another. Two herds were approaching one another from opposite sides of the valley, a short distance above our camp; and the master bulls were roaring defiance as they mustered their harems.

I walked stealthily up the valley, until I felt that I was nearly between the two herds; and then stood motionless under a tall pine. The ground was quite open at this point, the pines, though large, being scattered; the little brook ran with a strangled murmur between its rows of willows and alders, for the ice along its edges nearly skimmed its breadth. The stars paled rapidly, the gray dawn brightened, and in the sky overhead faint rose-colored streaks were turning blood-red. What little wind there was breathed in my face and kept me from discovery.

I made up my mind, from the sound of the challenging, now very near me, that one bull on my right was advancing towards a rival on my left, who was answering every call. Soon the former approached so near that I could hear him crack the branches, and beat the bushes with his horns; and I slipped quietly from tree to tree, so as to meet him when he came out into the more open woodland. Day broke, and crimson gleams played across the snow-clad mountains beyond.

At last, just as the sun flamed red above the hilltops, I heard the roar of the wapiti's challenge not fifty yards away; and I cocked and half raised my rifle, and stood motionless. In a moment more, the belt of spruces in front of me swayed and opened, and the lordly bull stepped out. He bore his massive antlers aloft; the snow lay thick on his mane; he snuffed the air and stamped on the ground as he walked. As I drew a bead, the motion caught his eye; and instantly his bearing of haughty and warlike self-confidence changed to one of alarm. My bullet smote through his shoulder-blades, and he plunged wildly forward, and fell full length on the blood-stained snow.

Nothing can be finer than a wapiti bull's carriage when excited or alarmed; he then seems the embodiment of strength and stately grace. But at ordinary times his looks are less attractive, as he walks with his neck level with his body and his head outstretched, his horns lying almost on his shoulders. The favorite gait of the wapiti is the trot, which is very fast, and which they can keep up for countless miles; when suddenly and greatly alarmed, they break into an awkward gallop, which is faster, but which speedily tires them.

I have occasionally killed elk in the neighborhood of my ranch on the Little Missouri. They were very plentiful along this river until 1881, but the last of the big bands were slaughtered or scattered about that time. Smaller bunches were found for two or three years longer; and to this day, scattered individuals, singly or in parties of two or three, linger here and there in the most remote and inaccessible parts of the broken country. In the old times they were often found on the open prairie, and were fond of sunning themselves on the sand bars by the river, even at midday, while they often fed by day-

In 1998, an estimated 500,000 elk ranged across much of the North American west and in pockets of the east and north. (Photo © Henry H. Holdsworth/Wild by Nature)

light (as they do still in remote mountain fastnesses). Nowadays the few survivors dwell in the timber of the roughest ravines, and only venture abroad at dusk or even after nightfall. Thanks to their wariness and seclusiveness, their presence is often not even suspected by the cowboys or others who occasionally ride through their haunts; and so the hunters only know vaguely of their existence. It thus happens that the last individuals of a species may linger in a locality for many years after the rest of their kind have vanished; on the Little Missouri to-day every elk (as in the Rockies every buffalo) killed is at once set down as "the last of its race." For several years in succession I myself kept killing one or two such "last survivors."

A yearling bull which I thus obtained was killed while in company with my staunch friend Will Dow, on one of the first trips which I took with that prince of drivers, old man Tompkins. We were laying in

our stock of winter meat; and had taken the wagon to go to a knot of high and very rugged hills where we knew there were deer, and thought there might be elk. Old Tompkins drove the wagon with unmoved composure up, down, and across frightful-looking hills, and when they became wholly impassable, steered the team over a cut bank and up a kind of winding ravine or wooded washout, until it became too rough and narrow for farther progress. There was good grass for the horses on a hill off to one side of us; and stunted cottonwood trees grew between the straight white walls of clay and sandstone which hemmed in the washout. We pitched our tent by a little trickling spring and kindled a great fire, the fitful glare lighting the bare cliffs and the queer, sprawling tops of the cottonwoods; and after a dinner of fried prairie-chicken went to bed. At dawn we were off, and hunted till nearly noon; when Dow, who had been walking to one side, beckoned

to me and remarked, "There's something mighty big in the timber down under the cliff; I guess it's an elk" (he had never seen one before); and the next moment, as old Tompkins expressed it, "the elk came bilin' out of the coulie." Old Tompkins had a rifle on this occasion and the sight of game always drove him crazy; as I aimed I heard Dow telling him "to let the boss do the shooting"; and I killed the elk to a savage interjectional accompaniment of threats delivered at old man Tompkins between the shots.

A bull elk on a frosty winter morning in Yellowstone National Park's Biscuit Basin. (Photo © Jeff and Alexa Henry)

THE GRASS GROWS HIGH

By Hal Borland

The late Hal Borland was a prolific journalist who wrote thousands of articles and editorials on nature subjects for many national publications, including hundreds of editorials for the *New York Times*. Les Line, former editor of *Audubon*, called him "the best naturalist in America." And writer and historian Barbara J. Mitchell wrote that Borland "speaks in a voice that resonates with the ancient rhythms of the life he so revered." In addition to his articles and editorials, he wrote more than thirty books for adults and children, including *High, Wide and Lonesome; When the Legends Die; King of Squaw Mountain; Hill Country Harvest; Wapiti Pete;* and *This Hill, This Valley.*

In this classic Borland piece, originally published in 1937 in *The American Magazine*, Borland tells the story of a majestic bull elk who gets the better of a pursuer who has little regard for the health of the land.

Cass Alexander told me the story of Old Pete, the bull elk of Squaw Mountain, one autumn afternoon as we sat on the stoop in front of his cabin and looked down across the gray green spruces and the naked, red-branched willows on the benchland. Far below us and to the east lay the Flats, a wasteland as far out as I could see, deep-gullied, rain-washed, windblown, with bunch grass struggling for a foothold.

"Some day," said Cass, "those Flats may be green again, if another Joe Selkirk doesn't move in. It'll be a long time, though. Grass that's gone stays gone a long time. And it goes in a hurry, once you put too many sheep on it. If it hadn't been for Old Pete," said Cass solemnly, "I'd like as not have another Death Valley right there in my front yard. Selkirk's sheep would have gnawed those Flats right down to sea level. It's only five thousand feet or so." He grinned and took a last puff at his pipe and told me about Pete. . . .

It was a cold spring, the season Pete was born, and the bull elk there in the shade of the Wind River range stayed in lower canyons long after they should have gone to the high benches. Usually the bulls quit the cows in March, when they've dropped their antlers and are feeling surly and ashamed of themselves.

"He'd seen many bulls in their prime, but few like this one, with a rack that gleamed white and had the mark of a monarch on every tine."—Hal Borland (Photo © Erwin and Peggy Bauer)

This year it was April, and when the cows trailed them toward high country they were beginning to calve, and the weaker cows were dying of the effort, so that the coyotes were following them like buzzards after a little bunch of thirst-blinded steers in midsummer.

They had got only as high as Juniper Bench when Pete was born, a gangling, big-headed, long-legged calf that had ears like a burro and a pelt like dead oak leaves with October moonlight filtered on them. Juniper Bench is like a shelf a third of the way up Squaw Mountain, where Granite Fork rests in deep pools before leaping into the canyon and where the grass in midsummer will make a horseman's spurs jingle. Pete was born there, and first felt the lick of his mother's rough tongue and lay in a world where even to breathe was a new experience. A chill wind blew through the brush, and the coyotes yapped; and the calf felt inner discomfort, which was hunger, and he nosed around till he found suckle. Then he slept, with the coyotes in the brush and the mountain lions in the rocks and the chill wind blowing.

The first few weeks of a calf's life are weeks of discovery, discovery of his legs, of his big ears, which catch sounds like funnels in the breeze, of his sensitive nose; discovery of other elk cows like his mother, which come and sniff at him and blow hot, grassy breath, and which kick unmercifully if he seeks food at their teats. He discovers grass, takes a few awkward mouthfuls and slobbers it out; he nibbles young oak leaves and finds them bitter, and he coughs at the tang of juniper fronds.

Pete grew, and June came, and July, and the calf's spots were fading, as his rump patch, almost absent at birth, began to whiten. Then August was there, with stifling hot days and hard-biting mountain flies and brush mosquitoes, so that there is no comfort in grazing and little comfort in rubbing through the brush, and relief only in splashing mud at a wallow stamped out at a seep-spring.

The herd was in a high valley, this August day, and the insects had finally driven one restless cow to the trail that led to such a mud-wallow at the foot of a cliff. As usual, the others followed, Pete's mother

A cow elk in a golden autumn field. (Photo © Jeff and Alexa Henry)

the third in line. But the calf, sensing the destination, pushed ahead, passed the next cow and the next, and trotted boldly up the trail. He had grown audacious but not yet wise.

He was perhaps ten yards in the lead when he came to the overhanging pine. A cow might have sensed the presence there, might have paused, perhaps turned aside. The calf did not even hesitate. And then a shadow blotted the trail. The mountain lion dropped, with only a little loosening of the bark from a limb, his claws splayed, his muscles set for the kill.

At that instant, however, the calf paused, flung up his head, flopped an ear to dislodge a fly. That fly saved his life. The calf halted. The cat jerked in mid-air, twisted desperately; and the calf leaped back. Instead of landing squarely on the calf's shoulders, bearing him to the ground, the lion stuck only a slashing blow with a splayed paw. One claw drove through the calf's ear, ripped it, laid open the shoulder.

The calf bawled once, almost as a terrified domestic calf might have, then spun on its hoofs and lunged away into the brush. And the sprawling cat, off balance, sprang after him too late. By then the cows had come up, stood startled; and the killer, snarling in rage, turned on them. . . . The herd lost two cows that afternoon. It saved a calf that would grow into a bull and a leader and a minor legend. . . .

That happened two summers before Cass came to Squaw Mountain; but to accuse Cass of romancing in his version of that incident would be ridiculous. Cass is a man who can look at a lion's track in the snow and state the brute's weight within five pounds, tell you its temper, even hazard a shrewd guess at the last time it fed. . . .

"You never knew Selkirk, did you?" Cass asked. "Well, the summer I came up here I stayed overnight at his place on the way in. Typical warm-weather sheep camp. Rambling log house and a string of corrals and a few sheds. If the wind was right you could smell it five miles away. It cost money to keep it clean, and Selkirk was the dollar-grabbing kind. Big fellow, he was; an old batch. Had an undershot jaw and a sandy beard and runover boots and greasy overalls. When I rode up he was out in the yard, with a pack of green-eyed dogs. Big, rough-haired brutes, part mastiff, part wolfhound, goodness knows what else.

"I hailed him, and he sized me up but didn't invite me to light and stay. 'Where you heading?' he asked.

"I'm not as touchy that way as some are. I told him and asked could he put me up for the night. 'I'm short of grub,' he said. 'You a trapper?' I admitted it. 'Well,' he said, 'for a dollar I'll put up you and your horses.' It was a scurvy way of doing, but I was tired and hungry. I told him to call off his pack. He picked up a club and they slunk away, hackles up and teeth bared. That's the way he handled his dogs.

"After supper Selkirk asked if I'd care to do some wolfing for him, at so much a scalp. I hesitated, and he said, 'I might make it worth your while to clean out the range robbers, too. Elk,' he explained. 'They're stealing my grass. One bunch especially, with an earmarked bull calf among 'em.'

"That's the first I heard of Pete.

"I reminded him that elk were protected.

"'Not when they're robbing range,' he said, and his eyes got kind of red.

"But I shook my head. I didn't care for his kind of law.

"'They're stealing grass,' Selkirk insisted, 'that'd feed a hundred thousand head of sheep.'

"'Government land, isn't it?' I asked.

"'No fence around it, is there?' he snorted. 'I'll clear 'em out and run my sheep in there. I'll put a hundred thousand head in there!'

"'Grass won't last long, that way,' I said.

"'You don't think grass lasts forever, do you?' he asked.

"'It does, if you treat it right. This you've been grazing down here was here long before you were born.'

"He glared. 'Who's going to stop me?'

"'Nobody,' I said, 'except maybe yourself.'

"He laughed, and it wasn't the kind of a laugh I care to sleep in the same room with. I went out and slept in the barn."

Cass didn't see Selkirk all that summer and fall,

After searching for forage on the edge of a pine forest, a bull pauses in the late October sunshine. (Photo © Daniel J. Cox/Natural Exposures, Inc.)

winter. They were still there in February. And Selkirk came out in February, with two helpers and a wagonload of ammunition. Cass rode down to see what all the shooting was about, and he found seventeen elk carcasses, all but three of them cows that would have calved in April. But he found no slit-eared bull among them.

He saw Selkirk, and the sheepman was ranting. Only the night before a band of elk, led by that slit-eared bull, had raided his camp and gored two horses so badly they had to be shot.

"I'll get him!" roared Selkirk. "I'll get him if it's the last thing I do. And I'll put enough sheep in here to eat every last blade of grass that bull ever sniffed at!"

When he left Selkirk, Cass circled the Flats, and in a foothill canyon far to the north he found Old Pete and six cows. He drove them deep into the hills, and kept them there. In two weeks Selkirk gave up and went back to bring in his sheep.

His sheep were so many that summer that when the wind was in the east Cass could smell them. The weather was ideal. The sheep fattened, and Selkirk was in a way to make a real fortune. He was heavily in debt, but half his huge flock would pay off his notes, the other half make him rich. July passed and August, and with the promise of a late fall he held the flocks there into September. Then caution got the better of greed and he cut the huge flock in half, sent the one half off to market with all but three of his herders. The remaining half he moved onto the last narrow band of grass there at the foot of Squaw Mountain.

It was a tableland there, not two miles wide and with a sharp canyon along its front and the first steep breaks of Squaw Mountain behind. Selkirk had kept that grass for this move. Here he would hold his own flock, fatten it fully while the sheep to pay off his debts went to market; and when he came back from the shipping, this flock would be ready for its last drive.

So he left them there, with three herders and that pack of dogs, and he hurried after the trail herd. He was gone six days.

It was the night before Selkirk returned that Cass heard the dogs. They were baying and they were in the meadows above Spruce Canyon. An hour later he heard them again, coming down from the ridges, over Juniper Bench. And still later he heard what was happening down on the tableland. He made a shrewd guess, and two days later he talked to one of the herders. That's how Cass knew.

The moon was late coming, that night, and the slit-eared bull and his cows fed contented until the deep baying of the dogs sounded far down the valley. The baying rose, and the elk calves stood close by their mothers, and the cows were restless. Old Pete stood apart, listening.

The deer led the dogs far up a distant ridge, finally gave them the slip. But after a time there was the sound of the dogs again. They had a new scent.

The elk moved away, lined out on a trail through the brush. All except Pete. He waited. The first dog loped into the clearing and set up his cry, and he made for the bull. He sprang, and Pete swept out with his antlers, and the dog yelped once and died. Then the rest of the pack poured into the open.

The buck knew his match. He took to the brush, away from his herd, the pack at his heels. Down the valley they drove him, out onto the tableland. And there were the sheep, bedded down.

The slit-eared bull raced through the grass, brittle with autumn, and he would have run, given his own way, to the steep canyon beyond and lost the dogs there. But the dogs were there at his heels, in full cry. The herders were roused; came out of their blankets blear-eyed and startled, and ran toward the flock. And, even as they ran, a skittish ewe leaped to her feet and fled headlong. Others followed, a long, crowding line of gray bodies.

The dogs drove the bull onward. To one side was that line of terrified sheep. To the other were the herders. Ahead lay the bulk of the flock, most of them bedded down like gray hummocks. And the bull, now baffled, plunged in among them.

They rose, then, wave on wave, with piteous bleating, and lunged at their neighbors. Ewes trampled lambs. Bucks trampled ewes. They piled up three deep. The stampede was on, and the canyon lay like a deep pool of black shadow ahead. . . .

Tule elk, once abundant in California's Sacramento and San Joaquin valleys, could not compete with livestock. Today, most of the remaining tule elk live on or near southern California's Tule Elk Refuge. (Photo © Jeffrey Rich)

Selkirk rode up from his camp late that after-noon, eager to look again on his flock. He must have been counting his dollars, one by one, and gloating at the way he had taken the wealth from those flats.

Then he came to the canyon, and he looked down and saw his flock, the flock that had poured over the wall like a flood in the moonlight. He paused there, and he cursed, and his eyes reddened with rage. Then he rode on, his rifle now in his hand.

One herder he found at the wagon, sitting dumbly and staring, mad-eyed, at the bedground. Selkirk paused and leaned over and cursed him, and the man fled, like a coyote. Selkirk shot at him, and missed. . . . One herder saw him coming and fled down the canyon. . . . The third herder told him what happened, covering Selkirk with his rifle meanwhile, and saying he'd as lief shoot the sheepman as breathe, if he made a false move. Selkirk went white, the herder later told Cass, when he said it was that bull with the slit ear which caused the stampede. Then he rode away, and he'd not got beyond rifle range when the herder heard the bugling of a bull elk far up the ridge. Selkirk reined up and listened. Then he headed up the mountain.

"I saw him," said Cass. "He passed right down there by that big pine, so close I could hear the creak of his saddle. Then that bull back on the ridge bugled again, and Selkirk rose in his stirrups and waved his gun in the air and yelled like an Indian.

"I followed his trail the next day and traced every step. He went up the ridge till he came to the edge of Juniper Bench. There his horse gave out and he cut through the brush on foot. Over at the far side of the Bench he came in sight of the bull, between three and four hundred yards away. Selkirk drew down on him and fired one shot. I found the cartridge. He hit the bull, knocked him down. But it wasn't a vital shot. Maybe it creased him. I don't know. Anyway, Selkirk ran on up thinking he had his crazy revenge.

"But before he got there the bull was up again, and running. Selkirk fired two more shots, close to-gether. I heard them. But he was crazy-mad, and his sights were still set high. The bull kept right on go-ing.

"Selkirk was crazy as a coot. He went tearing up the slope, and the bull there in front of him, going up too.

The bugle of a powerful bull is something to savor. (Photo © Erwin and Peggy Bauer)

Above: *An alert Rocky Mountain bull resting in a field. (Photo © John W. Herbst)*

Right: *Bulls will bugle in response to the call of a nearby bull in an attempt to "out-advertise" the other bull and win the favor of cows. (Photo © Doug Locke)*

Above: *A majestic bull on the edge of a mountain forest. (Photo © Michael Mauro)*
Overleaf: *The sun goes down over wapiti country. (Photo © Jeff and Alexa Henry)*

"That slope was steep as a roof, and mostly loose rock carried down by a snow slide a long time ago, with a scattering of boulders in it. Selkirk got about halfway up, and the bull was near the top. Then it happened. The bull possibly deliberately nudged a loose boulder, and that one hit a couple more. Before you could say scat, there was as fine a rock slide as you'll ever see. Selkirk was right in the middle of it."

Cass tamped his pipe and held a match to it. Then he stared off to the east.

"We buried him," he said, "with his sheep, there in the canyon."

"And the bull?" I asked.

Cass went inside and came back with a piece of elk antler, a three-pointed prong that had been cut off with a bullet.

"I picked that up," Cass said, "where the bull would have been when Selkirk fired those two shots together. I told you he was shooting high. . . . Two weeks after it happened I was back on the ridge and I spotted a herd down on the Bench. I put the binoculars on them, and there was Old Pete, slit-ear and white scar on his shoulder and all. Then I looked at his rack. The right antler was shy three prongs at the tip. . . . I'd have given a pretty to have found those antlers when he dropped them the next spring. I'd liked to have taken them down to Selkirk's old place and nailed them over the door, and left them there till the walls fall in and the logs rot and the grass grows high, like it used to."